A VIEW FROM THE BACKHOE

A VIEW FROM THE BACKHOE

It's about Attitude!

Mike Gaymon

Mike Gaymon

ISBN: 1517719119
ISBN 13: 9781517719111
Library of Congress Control Number: 2015916757
CreateSpace Independent Publishing Platform
North Charleston, South Carolina

Contents

Foreward

M ost of us go through challenges and opportunities that can test us emotionally, physically, financially, and spiritually. Perhaps you have heard many times, as I have, about the importance of our own attitudes when things happen to us.

Life is full of moments, both good and bad, from which we can grow and learn. Personally, I do not believe in good luck. Instead, I believe that one can make his/her own luck by hard work, by preparation, and by allowing himself to be guided by a "higher spiritual being". In my life, that is God.

This book is not about religion or about trying to convert anyone to my beliefs. It is however, about some personal and professional challenges and opportunities that I have encountered and lessons learned from them.

It is about stories in my life.

You can read one chapter and put this book down for an hour, a day, or a week, and pick it back up and read another in a few minutes. It is not fiction and certainly not intended to be a novel. Instead, it recaps some stories in my life that have helped mold me in my thinking and actions.

Like the clay on a potter's wheel, it is through "the shaping process" that we can become molded. Sometimes painful, it also can be truly exciting when the wheel stops spinning.

There are many people who have helped to shape and mold me... my family, teachers, friends, as well as some really excellent leaders with whom I have had the opportunity to work. I have truly been blessed, both personally and professionally, by people who cared enough to give their time, talents, and input to me. Even when I might not have deserved it, they never gave up; and in turn, that helped me to never give up.

Of course, there are those who had their own egos and agendas that seemed to only care about themselves and tear down rather than build. Even those, whom I would like to forget, did their part in helping to shape me. Isn't it ironic that sometimes the people or instances that are so painful, so hurtful, also have their places in our shaping and our molding! But, isn't that life? It is not about what knocks us down, but about what picks us up, and what we become, having gone through the experience, that really counts.

I believe that our attitude governs our altitude.

One of my wife's favorite cities is Charleston, SC. Obviously, the historical aspects of the city are truly unique and wonderful to see. However, one of the things that we like about the city of Charleston is a restaurant known as Hyman's Seafood. They have a motto that is printed on much of their marketing materials that is as great, to me, as their wonderful seafood. It was written by Dr. Chuck Swindoll and is below:

"The longer I live, the more I realize the impact of attitude on life. Attitude, to me, is more important than education, than money, than circumstances, then failures, than successes, than what other people think or say or do. It is more important than appearance, giftedness, or skill. It will make or break a company...a church...a home. The remarkable thing is we have a choice everyday regarding the attitude we embrace for that day. We cannot change our past... we cannot change the fact that people act in a certain. We cannot change the inevitable. The only thing we can do is play on the one string we have and that is our attitude...I am convinced that life is

10% what happens to me and 90% how I react to it. And so it is with you…we are in charge of our ATTITUDES."

This book is written from that perspective. Hopefully, it will encourage, enlighten, and perhaps bring some positive reflection to make the reader's life just a little bit better.

A View from the Backhoe

It's funny the things that come to mind when I'm trying to do anything but think.

Cleaning the leaves, limbs, dirt, and mud from the ditches after spring rains is a yearly job. The winter rains bring down lots of debris that clog the ditches and keep the water from flowing freely into the ponds. All of this thick muck gets so compacted that I can't dig out so much as a shovel full without straining my back.

We call it "The Country".

It's a house my wife, Sheila, and I built back in 2000. It's the kind of place you couldn't find unless you were looking for it … and sometimes not even then. There's the house and a pond stocked full of catfish, small-mouth bass, bream, and much to my endless frustration and occasional fussing, carp nearly as big around as a grown man's thigh. We've got acreage surrounded by nothing but open fields, pine trees, and blue skies.

The Country is so far out that cell phones can't reach me. Until a few months ago, there was no email, no Wi-Fi, and no internet-- free from instant contact and a real get a-way. There are no people, unless the family is there for a visit, so the solitude is refreshing.

Sheila and I go there whenever we can. Since I have retired after 38.5 years working as a Chamber of Commerce President at various places in South & North Carolina, Alabama, and Georgia, including over 26 years as CEO of the Columbus, Georgia Chamber of Commerce, those chances to get away from the city are coming more and more often.

Up there, I can get back to my country roots. After a 38-year career of answering the calls and demands of mayors, city council members, business owners, civic leaders, and those concerned citizens who reach out a friendly hand and a sweet smile every time I sit down to dinner at every restaurant in town, it's nice to have a place where nobody wants anything. However, all of that was part of my job and had tremendous benefits of being in the center of lots of issues and discussions. Of course, now that I have retired, most of those handshakes and smiles are offered to say how much they miss me, and that's something I would never complain about; and I greatly appreciate it.

In The Country, I can clean the cobwebs out of my mind by getting sweat in my eyes, blisters on my fingers, mud in my shoes and a deep pain in my back. It is the kind of place where the only person I have got to please is myself, and the woods and fish in the ponds are the only things paying any attention to the work I do.

The soil in Harris County can get as thick as Play Doh. I have put my back in spasms at times by just pulling up a shovel full of that dirt; and most of the time it was just a wet glob of muck and mud that stuck to the shovel better than any glue invented by man.

I decided I needed a backhoe to do the work a shovel could not and a 60 plus-year-old man just should not do. After months of looking, most of the backhoes I came across were so old and so worn out they should have been sent out to rust in a junk yard. Buying one would have been a waste of time and money.

Finally, an old friend and fellow grown-up country boy, Jerry Booker, who owns property in Harris County said he had a backhoe to sell. It was old, but it had been maintained well. Ever since I bought it, that Ol' Backhoe has been the perfect assistant. She is never too tired and will do whatever I ask; but I have got to take it easy with her, remembering her age and my lack of experience.

I know my way around a shovel, but a backhoe – even one with this many years of wear and tear– requires a certain finesse that I have yet to master; so when she starts to buck, moan and groan, I just use my most soothing, reassuring preacher's son's voice to calm both her and me down, remembering that neither of us is as young as we used to be. I cannot get in too much of a hurry because if that Ol' Backhoe gives out on me, it will be back to the shovel.

So there I was, sitting on the Ol' Backhoe, ready to dig out the ditches so the water could flow freely. It was a beautiful day with a slight breeze. There were no phones, no emails, no people … just a man and his machine ready to do some digging.

As I lowered the bucket into the dirty water, reaching down to the bottom of the ditch, I could tell that there was a lot of debris. The Ol' Backhoe groaned from the load, but she pulled through like she had so many times before and continues to do still. After a couple more loads, the water began to flow through the pipe and into the pond. As the debris was cleared, what started as a little swirl steadily grew into a flow.

Watching the water move, free and clear, I realized how the debris that backhoe moved was much like the chapters in my life. There have been many things that clogged my thoughts, feelings, and dreams.

There was the debris from the divorce in 1988.

In my family, marriage was for life. There was nothing that could not be overcome, nothing that could destroy the union of a husband and wife. However, as so often is the case with divorce, everything changed. The family was broken apart. A planned move from Anniston, Ala. to Columbus, Ga. – a move that was going to be a new chapter for our family – became a journey I made alone.

Dreams vanished, some changed shape, and others became more debris.

Our little girls, Sumer, 11, Robin, 8, and Kasey, 5, were caught in the middle. I never thought my children would grow up living with their Mom in one state and their Dad in another.

I'll never forget – or forgive - the counselor saying that my oldest daughter, who was only 12 at the time was "under too much pressure to visit me every other weekend." What? Doesn't being with her Dad, even if it's only for a couple of weekends a month, give her the opportunity for a better relationship? The divorce was going to be hard enough as it was – the distance, the separation, the confusion – and now, I was supposed to be a father who rarely saw his daughter. The courts and lawyers sided with their mother, leaving me with little choice but to make the best of it.

Sitting on the backhoe on that beautiful spring day, I watched as the water begin to flow; and I drifted back through those dark, lonesome, and challenging days. The debris from that time had taken its toll, not only on me, but also on those three little girls who have each grown into women with lives, children, and debris of their own. I thought too much about what could have been. I questioned what I could have done differently. I had some very candid questions for God. I wanted to know why … why me?

I have finally accepted that there are things that I cannot change. Even with all of my efforts, the outcome, at least of the marriage, was beyond my control. Though so much had been taken away, only I could decide the kind of father I was going to be – no matter the divorce or the distance. My daughters were going to know that their Dad would always be there for them, whatever the future held.

All these years later, it's a promise that I like to think I have kept. Despite the debris that has gotten in the way, the girls and I have always managed to clear the way back to each other.

Then, I think about the parents who have lost a child in an accident or to some kind of disease and it puts some things in perspective. I have never had that kind of pain and hope to God that I never will. Whatever the circumstances, most people experience gut wrenching things in life that can cut them down to the very core of their souls.

It is real. It can take every bit of the life and breath out of you, and rightly so. The bottom line to these kinds of hurts and pain is what happens afterwards. Do they make us stronger and wiser or only wounded and hurt?

Sitting on that Ol' Backhoe, I thought about all the other debris that had clogged up my life over the years – the conflicts, the decisions, the choices, the deadlines, the controversies, and the second-guesses. I knew there was a power greater than all of my abilities and efforts; and all I needed to do was to trust in God, to have faith, and to know that He would remove the debris from my life.

Funny, the things you think about when you're trying not to think at all. Pretty much the answers to all my problems – then, now, and tomorrow – were pouring out right there in front of me. The stagnant water was flowing out; the fresh water was trickling in through those freshly dug ditches, and in my head, I was humming – "Springs of Living Water" - an old hymn Dad used to have the family sing:

Drinking at the springs of living water
Happy now am I, my soul is satisfied
Drinking at the springs of living water
O wonderful and bountiful supply
How sweet the living water from the hills of God
It makes me glad and happy all the way
Now glory, grace, and blessing mark the path I've trod
I'm shouting "Hallelujah" every day

Sometimes, our own living springs can become stagnant. The water that should bring us life and joy is undrinkable, even poisonous.

The more water that flowed through those ditches, the wider I smiled. My heart was flooded with pleasant thoughts and happy memories. Sitting on that Ol' Backhoe that I had bought from a friend to save me from a whole lot of back pain had not only cleared up some debris in a ditch, but it gave me the perspective to see how God had cleared some debris from my own life.

As Paul Harvey used to say, "Now, the rest of the story". When I got much of the old stuff out of my personal ditch, the fresh, new water started to flow and has been flowing ever since. The relationship with my three daughters is stronger than ever, now that they're adults. I met Sheila, a wonderful, caring woman who has become the rock in my life. We were married over 21 years ago. She, along with my faith in God, has been a source of strength and comfort for me and for my girls.

With the new flow of water came Sheila's sons, Bill and Wes, my two "bonus sons". There also came her brother, Larry, a unique guy who knows something about almost everything. My additional family, thanks to Sheila and her family and friends, has made me a truly blessed man.

I can't leave out Sheila's mother's three sisters...Lois, Christine, and Loretta (Annie, Tine, and Retta to us). They are the hardest working women I have ever seen. They also add a lot of color to the family. All three of them are great cooks; and if we compliment on a dish and ask who made it, all three of them will raise their hands and take credit. It's a family filled with a lot of laughter.

So, clearing out "my ditches" made room for the fresh water to flow into my life. Instead of some stale and stagnant water, there was an abundance of fresh water bringing life and joy to myself and others. I will never forget my morning on the Ol' Backhoe, nor the life lessons that marked me for life on that sunny, digging day.

I also remember thinking that if I ever got around to writing a book about my life and the lessons I have learned along the way, I would have to be sure to include a story about that Ol' Backhoe in there. People just might like that sort of thing. It might help someone to look into their own ditches and do some digging.

Sometimes Love Isn't Enough

No amount of love can overcome an absolute commitment to achieve. The love of the game can push someone to train, to practice, and to achieve. Some of the greatest feats in sports have come from more than just the love of the game.

Bill Crompton was in the 1963 Olympics. The critics said that he was too slow to actually be in the Olympics, but in race after race he was able to get into the next heat; and there he was in the finals of the 800 meter race.

Toward the end of the race, Bill's lead was fading. It became a photo finish. As the individual frames of the photos were being reviewed, someone noticed that Bill appeared to be saying something. They put all the photos together; and they found that Bill was saying, "I want to win. I want to win."

The love that his family had for him and his love for the sport certainly got him to be in the position of being in the Olympics. Perhaps, his determination, his absolute refusal to lose, was what drove him across the finish line to the victory. Love can take you a long way; but in the end, it may not be enough to win.

We can learn a lot from Mother Nature. Geese, for example, fly in a "V" formation. There are many positive things that contribute to this formation and natural actions of the geese.

1. The formation gains a 71% greater flying range; when a goose falls out of formation, it quickly feels the drag and resistance

and gets back into formation to gain the lifting power of the other birds.

2. When the leading goose gets tired, it rotates back in the "V" to let another one lead for a while.

3. The geese honk regularly to encourage the flock to keep flying.

4. When one goose gets sick or falls out, often another one will fall out of formation with it to help it or stay with it, either until it gets better, or dies.

Is it love or just Mother Nature that causes the geese to respond in these ways? Perhaps, if we cared more for each other by encouraging rather than tearing down, our world would be different. What if we tried to find common ground, rather than my way is the only way? Taking turns and allowing others to contribute and be a part can make a real difference. Finding ways to stick together and help each other out when we ourselves are really in need of help can be therapeutic.

Maybe love is not enough. Maybe we need to learn from Mother Nature to do the right things for the right reasons without strings being attached. Perhaps, for the majority of people, there is a built in trigger of knowing right from wrong. You do not have to love someone to be a good person and treat people fairly.

To suggest that love could ever fail or fall short sounds contradictory to the faith and core values that I have laid out in these pages; but before discarding such a heartbreaking idea, reflect on your own life, to a time when, in spite of your best efforts, things happened that caused hurt, anger, and disappointments…love simply was not enough.

It's like the Darryl Worley country song about a man who has been called to pull his buddy out of the bar, where he is drinking his bad luck away. When he asks his friend what is going on, he responds with, "Sarah's old car's about to fall apart, and the washer quit last week. We had to put momma in the nursing home and the baby's cutting teeth. I didn't get much work this week, and I got bills to pay." After listening to all his friend's troubles, the man, not without patience, but a little short of sympathy, responds, simply, "Sounds like life to me…"

There is a lot of wisdom in that country song.

Things happen, good and bad. We need to adjust and find a way to work through the hard times. The more we struggle, the stronger we will be when we come out on the other side. Sure, it is easy to say, but it is pretty hard to do when you are stuck in the middle of one of those "sounds like life" situations.

Have you ever worked as hard as you can work, only to find that there is no light at the end of the tunnel, even after all your hard work? It can be demoralizing and frustrating.

I love dogs. I have had one—sometimes more than one—pretty much all of my life. Dogs know only unconditional love. Whenever those Humane Society commercials come on TV, showing dogs that have been abused, abandoned, left to fend for themselves, starving, unloved, and unwanted, I turn the channel. Those eyes seem to hold all the sorrow and hurt of the world. Knowing that each one is filled to bursting with that unconditional love, yet has not found a home to share is too much. Call me soft-hearted, but it is how I feel.

Everyone should know that kind of love.

One day while driving to Atlanta for a meeting, I saw something in the road ahead. At first, I thought it was a deer someone had hit and killed during the night; but as I got closer, I could tell that it was not one animal, but two. Something was lying in the road, and there was another animal standing over it.

There were two dogs. One was dead, apparently having been hit by a car; and the other dog was nuzzling at his companion, trying to help his friend up; but it was too late. I had to pull over to watch this sad, yet profound, expression of love.

No matter how he tried; no matter how much he pushed and pulled to get his friend up and out of the road, his love for his friend just was not enough to bring him back to life. There would be no miracles on this day, but the dog did not understand. He only knew that he was now alone.

Watching that heartbroken dog, I could not help but think about the number of times that I have pushed and pulled with all my strength, with my entire being, only to find that it just was not enough…that my love was not enough.

We have all been through such a time. If you are a parent, maybe it is watching as a child's marriage falls apart. The dreams you had for him/her – of being happy with a family of his/her own, finding someone to share the rest of his/her life with—has faded away, replaced by a harsh reality of pain, regret, and starting over. Love is not enough to prevent or repair this decision that will ripple through generations.

Parents, who find themselves suddenly single, understand the disappointment that comes with loving someone who, no matter what you did or said, nothing could mend what had been torn apart at the seams. They made a decision that impacted you and there was nothing that could have been done to change his/her mind. It is a sick, empty feeling that reaches down to the bottom of your soul.

What do we do when our love is not enough?

There are choices. Sometimes the painful lessons are the most valuable because they are the ones we carry around for the longest time. We can learn from the experience – good and bad – making sure that we take insight from both to guide us through relationships in the future; or we can accept defeat and remember only the bad things. However, to do that means you are not growing from the experiences, which often means you will be doomed to repeat the same mistakes over and over again, never knowing why.

I watched that dog on the road and thought about all the times my love was not enough. I watched until he accepted that his friend was not coming back, that he was not getting off the road, and that he would have to make his way alone. I watched until he finally disappeared into the nearby woods.

As I drove away I wondered about the things I could have said differently. What if I had made a different decision? If I could do it all over again, what would I change? And, the hardest question of all, would it have mattered if I had?

Sounds like life to me. Things happen. No matter what we say or do, some things work out, some things don't, but at times nothing goes according to plan.

Sometimes love may not be enough, but it may be all we have to give.

Monday Morning Quarterbacking

The Monday Morning Quarterback is always right.

You do not have to be a football fan to appreciate the Monday Morning Quarterback; but, for the sake of those who may not know football terminology, here is a layman's explanation: The Monday Morning Quarterback is someone who uses the passage of time and past events to second-guess the decision of another, using his input to prove what should have been done. Think of the Monday Morning Quarterback in terms of another popular cliché – hindsight is always 20/20.

It is an enviable position, that of the Monday Morning Quarterback, because he always knows the decision that *should have* been made; and oh, how he likes to point this out.

Everyone knows the Monday Morning Quarterback---I have known many.

There have been more times than I can count when, a day or two after a decision was made, there would be a comment – either in the newspaper, in a meeting, or just idle conversation – about what *could* have or *should* have been done. Of course, those comments were based on additional facts or circumstances that brought further details to light (information that I did not have at that point in time) but the Monday Morning Quarterback was able to use after the fact.

It is easy to criticize and second guess, but it is tougher to act.

I live in Columbus, Georgia, where college football is king. From August to January, football is all many people talk about; and it is almost all they talk about the other six months of the year. With the University of Georgia, Georgia Tech, Auburn, and the University of Alabama all within driving distance, this part of the South is teeming with football rivalries. From the community coffee pot just before Sunday church service, to the Coke machines at the office on Friday, there is not a day that goes by after the games when the Monday Morning Quarterback, who always plays for the losing team, is not willing to share his or her opinion on what went wrong on the field that Saturday.

Vince Dooley knows a thing or two about the Monday Morning Quarterback.

"Coach Dooley" as everybody knows him, spent 25 years with the University of Georgia, where he won six SEC championships and a national championship in 1980. In this part of the country, that means he is a legend who never has to worry about paying for his own drink. However, even legends have to deal with the Monday Morning Quarterback.

Coach Dooley shared a story with the Columbus Rotary Club in 2014, which taught me all I needed to know about dealing with those who insist on second-guessing me after the real work has already been done.

In the mid-1960's in one of Coach Dooley's first seasons as head coach of UGA, the "Dawgs" were playing rival Clemson Tigers on Georgia's home field. Clemson had pinned Georgia back on the one-inch line of their own end zone. Coach Dooley tried to catch Clemson off guard by calling a quarterback sweep, where the football is snapped to the quarterback, who runs to the outside of most of the offensive line and down the sideline, hopefully for a big gain. It is a gutsy call that is usually run at midfield or deeper because the quarterback can just as easily be tackled for a loss.

Clemson was not caught by surprise; and Georgia's quarterback was tackled in his own end zone, giving Clemson not only two points with the safety, but they got the ball back on the ensuing kickoff, which Clemson eventually took in for another touchdown, winning the game.

Georgia fans were heartbroken, angry, and more than a little upset at their young coach. Losing to anybody is bad; losing to Clemson at home was almost unforgivable.

The following Monday, Coach Dooley was having lunch with the university president. As he was about to leave, the president offered Coach Dooley some unsolicited advice, prefacing it with, "Normally, I would not offer my opinion…but when you have the ball on your one-inch line, it is not a good idea to run a quarterback sweep."

Without hesitation, Coach Dooley responded, telling the president of the University of Georgia if he had been given several days to think about it – much as the president obviously had been—he would not have called a quarterback sweep either.

When telling this story, Coach Dooley was quick to add that back when he was young, he would often say whatever was in his mind without thinking about the consequences, which could have easily gotten a young coach in trouble. Fortunately, he went on to become the longest and most successful football coach the University of Georgia has ever had; and after that, he went on to become a beloved and respected athletic director at UGA for nearly 25 years.

After he shared this story with Rotary Club, I thought of some of my own play calling and the times when I made a decision, only to have various "Monday Morning Quarterbacks" offer their own input as to what I *should have* done. However, at the time, a decision needed to be made, based on the facts with which I (as well as my staff) had to work.

One of the problems when facing the Monday Morning Quarterbacks of the world is not trying too hard to defend the decision they are second guessing. Do that, and you will just sound defensive, thus justifying their criticism. The last thing you want is the Monday Morning Quarterback thinking you are only interested in covering your own behind.

This is not to say that what the Monday Morning Quarterback has to say is all bad. For one thing, you can learn from him/her what not to do the next time a similar situation arises by having the voice of the Monday Morning Quarterback in your head before making a decision, hearing all the ways something can –and so often will—go wrong. Experience, or in this instance, failure, can be an excellent teacher, even as it bruises the ego. Imagine how the course of history might have been changed had someone only listened to the Monday Morning Quarterback!

How many times must the Children of Israel have second guessed Moses--- Why did you bring us here to this barren land when we had homes back in Egypt? What are we going to do now that we are stuck at the Red Sea and the Pharaohs' chariots are chasing us? Soon, they will catch us and either kill us or take us back to live as slaves in Egypt. If you know your Bible, you know how things worked out. It took 40 years of the Israelites' wandering through Egypt and generations beyond before they knew true freedom.

As leaders, as parents, and as members of a community, one of our challenges today is to avoid falling prey to the Monday Morning Quarterback. They will be quick to let you know their opinions and their decisions, if only they had been given the chance to make them, but those opinions are based solely on hindsight, something that those of us making the actual decisions do not have the luxury of using. We make decisions because the circumstances warrant it.

As a parent or grandparent, we make many decisions and choose courses of action that can be life changing. As difficult as they are, deciding *not* to decide, deciding *not* to do *anything*, is still a decision.

No matter the outcome, we have to look in the mirror and into the eyes of those who trusted us with the responsibility and know that we did our best.

So, get ready when your teenager comes back with some Monday Morning Quarterback insight aimed at proving just how you blew it. Get ready when your grown child offers his/her input to show how he/she was right, and you were wrong. We all know raising children is not easy. They do not come with instructions on what to do and when to do it; but that cannot keep us from calling the plays and living with the results.

As managers, we should be ready to deal with the Monday Morning Quarterback's feedback. It just comes with the territory. Our challenge is deciding what to do with the input when it comes. We also need to learn from it in order to help everyone else involved…not just ourselves.

We are expected to make the tough calls. We are not allowed to take the easy way out, the short cut; and, we take the blame from the Monday Morning Quarterbacks when things did not turn out like we had promised. We cannot have 100 percent success with every play. That is why it is helpful to remember that no one is perfect. Everyone makes mistakes.

Those Monday Morning Quarterbacks are usually legends in their own minds and that is where they will stay…in their own minds.

4

Beware of the First Report

Much has been written about leadership. I have read many articles, publications, and speeches about leadership. This chapter is a summary of many that I have found to be inspirational and useful, both professionally and personally.

When I worked for the Columbus Georgia Chamber of Commerce we had a program we called the Total Resource Campaign. Each week of the campaign we asked various leaders to give a summary of the key leadership elements they had found to be helpful to them in their careers.

Lt. Gen. (Ret.) Carmen Cavezza was one of our guest speakers. He had a great career in the Army, becoming a Lt. General, a rank of which few Army people ever achieve. He also ran the Olympic Fast Pitch Softball event in Columbus back in 1996. Many people said that this venue in Columbus was one of the best venues of all the Olympic Games, and I believe one of the main reasons for such success was due to Carmen's leadership.

Gen. Cavezza told us that when he was in the Army, hundreds of people followed his commands, but leading civilian volunteers was entirely different. These civilian volunteers of the Olympics would ask questions about his suggestions, something to which he was not accustomed. It was not at all like commanding in the Army. Carmen said he felt like a cemetery superintendent; he was over a lot of folks, but none of them paid attention.

Carmen also served as the first Sports Council Director of Columbus and later became the City Manager, using his PhD in Government. Following his retirement as City Manager, he was the Director of the Cunningham Center for Leadership at Columbus State University.

So, to say that Carmen had experienced and knew a lot about leadership is a gross understatement! The man knows about leadership!

We all have found ourselves hearing a report or a recap of a conversation. The natural, and perhaps instinctive, thing to do is to react. Based on it, we can form our opinions and begin to think about a way to respond. However, one of the key elements of Carmen's presentation was to NEVER TOTALLY BELIEVE THE FIRST REPORT.

In reflecting on my 40-plus years of work, there were many times I could have benefitted from taking this advice instead of not doing so. For example, a staff member would tell me of a conversation he/she had heard and then share his/her interpretations of what was said; or a family member might call and tell me of something going on with someone else in the family. As a Type A personality, I was often ready to spring into action. While my intentions were good, immediate action was not always the best way to remedy the problem.

My failure did not come due to a lack of ideas. It was not due to a knee jerk reaction, without regard to past experiences. Instead, it was because the first report did not provide the whole picture; and more pieces were needed to complete the puzzle. There is nothing wrong with taking some time to consider and process the information.

For example, when one of my daughters came in with a story about something that happened to her, it was generally full of the drama and typical energy that seems to fuel the average child or teenager. After listening to her and telling her that I needed to think about it a little more, she seemed all right for the time being. Later, she would share more information about what had happened, and this invariably changed the way I responded. Based upon that additional input, the course of response was altered.

Of course, things like that happen often from the standpoint of children telling their versions of a story as they remembered it at the time. However, what really is discouraging is when the "big people" tell their versions of an account, only to find out later that the input that you received was only part of the story.

There is a Latin phrase that says, "Illegitimi non carborundum". The translation of that Latin phrase is, "Don't let the bastards grind you down."

One of the greatest people that I have ever known was Howard "Bo" Callaway. He was a great American, an amazing advocate for nature, an excellent businessman, and a wonderful friend to me.

His parents founded Callaway Gardens, one of the finest gardens of its kind in the United States, about 45 minutes south of Atlanta, Georgia, and 35 miles from Columbus, Georgia.

Bo was the first Republican Congressman from Georgia since Reconstruction and would have been the state's first Republican Governor in 1966, had it not been for some clever maneuvering by the State Democratic Party. He later became the Secretary of the Army.

Bo invited my wife, Sheila, and me to his condo for dinner. He went into his bedroom and brought back a sign with the Latin words inscribed…"Illegitimi non carborundum". The sign was given to him by his staff when he was the Secretary of the Army. During that time, he was accused by most of the main stream media of taking kickbacks from defense contractors. For many weeks, this was a lead story on or near the front page of the newspapers. Finally, after being accused of wrong doing and having his good name plastered all over the media, the final report of the "witch hunt" came out to state that there was NO (zero) evidence of anything that he had done that was improper or dishonest.

He ended that story by telling me that the final disclosure of the investigation was put far back in the national newspapers as a very small article. Instead of the equal treatment and exposure of the story from when the political lead investigation was started, it ended with barely a mention. If people read the first press reports, then, Bo was already guilty before any investigation was ever conducted. That same attitude continues today. Many leaders find themselves in the "cross hairs", being a target. The First Reports can be very damning and hurtful. Often, when the final investigating is done, the final report can be totally different from what the first reports indicated.

Bo knew that at that particular time there were some folks who were trying to ruin my name and reputation. He wanted to share history with me because he cared. He also told me that he wanted to encourage me to not give in to the pressures and people with their own agendas, but to be myself and not to let them get me down.

I will never forget Bo's sharing his story about the first reports with me that night. He encouraged me and challenged me to stay on the high road and to not let them get me down. He also warned me that the "First Reports" will usually get the most coverage, whether or not they are correct.

Thanks, Bo, for your friendship and your words of wisdom. I shall never forget them.

Working for a volunteer organization was wonderful, but also challenging. We depended upon volunteers to chair committees and to be an active part of the organization. My staff had free access to any and all of the volunteers. Usually, that created a great working environment. However, there were a few times a staff person decided to go against a decision and run to selected volunteers to "cry on their shoulders". I could understand it when the "Type A Personality", who was driven and did not like to lose, resorted to this. I did not support it, and in fact, tried to discourage it from a team building standpoint for the staff and volunteers. However, there were a few times when a few of the volunteers believed the "First Report". Instead of listening and encouraging the staff person to have a heart to heart talk with me, they would listen, counsel, and sometimes support the staff member.

I do not think that the volunteers were doing it with any malice intent or with thought of undermining my leadership. However, I believe that if they had not taken the "First Report" as the absolute and had taken more time to understand and question to find out directly for themselves, there would not have been some of the challenges that occurred. Imagine how much time, talent, and resources have been wasted by reacting to that dangerous "First Report". These instances took energy away from the organization, including both staff and volunteers.

Reflecting on those few incidents helped me to be cautious of my acceptance of the "First Report" from staff or volunteers. It surely helped me to move through many issues without being bogged down with a firm position too early.

In chamber business, the first report often sounded awful. A volunteer was upset and was threatening to cancel a membership; but after a little time passed since the "First Report", the facts were uncovered; and the potentially bad situation was resolved.

It is also very important to make sure that you have a clear understanding of what is supposed to be communicated. During one of the terrible hurricanes in South Louisiana, a local television station asked a woman how such complete devastation of the churches in the area had affected the lives of the people in the area. Without hesitation, the woman replied, "I don't know about the other people, but we haven't gone to Church's in years. We get our chicken from Popeye's." So, clarity can also be a very important ingredient in receiving the "First Report".

Of course, there are times when an instant response is necessary. There are times when we do not have the luxury of time and information-gathering. During those times, the past experiences of responding to the "First Report" can serve as a good guide on how to respond in a moment of professional or personal crisis.

However, most of the time, the smart thing to do is to take a step back, consider the options, wait for the whole picture to appear; and then decide what to do next because the "First Report" is rarely the last report.

5

Stamp Collecting

S&H Green Stamps were a type of trading stamp that allowed, or enabled, those of us who grew up in the 60's and 70's to have a few "luxuries" (extras) that we might not have had, otherwise. There were other types of trading stamps, but my family saved Green Stamps from the local Winn Dixie.

When we bought groceries from Winn Dixie, the cashier gave us Green Stamps that were the equivalent to the amount of groceries we bought. So, $25 worth of groceries were equal to $25 in Green Stamps.

We licked the stamps and stuck them in collection books. The books were traded in for merchandise, such as household goods and furniture, etc. I do not know what kind of glue was used on the back of the stamps; but after a couple of licks, it was almost impossible to get rid of that taste. Today, that paste would probably be banned by the FDA, and Dr. Phil would be doing a special hour on its dangers. However, back then, well…let's just say kids had more things to worry about than ingesting glue from green stamps.

In our house, those Green Stamps were a big deal. Heaven help me if I went to the grocery store and forgot to get the stamps. As soon as I told Momma that I had forgotten to get the stamps, I knew I was going right back to the store, receipt in hand, to claim those stamps. After riding my bike the 20 minutes it took to get to Winn Dixie – the second time—I stopped forgetting the stamps.

The stamps were important to my family because we were a poor family; and we redeemed those books at the S&H Redemption Store for merchandise that we normally could not afford and would not have spent money on, even if we could have. Depending upon how many books of stamps we had, we could get merchandise for them. Things…like an electric blanket. Talk about a luxury!

When I was a kid, the closest thing my older brother, Hal, and I had to a heated blanket on those cold South Carolina nights was when we would hold our blankets in front of the coal stove and run back to bed to curl up under it before it cooled off again.

Daddy was not happy that Momma used those stamps to purchase an electric blanket, which he figured would eventually electrocute them. Of course, I was not too worried about being electrocuted because I knew that blanket was not going anywhere near my bed.

Why anyone would want one of those things was something Daddy just could not understand. He would say the same thing about some of the other stuff we bought with those stamps, like a Brownie camera; but since we did not have to pay for them, Daddy did not complain too much.

Fast forward into my career. If you are someone who is trying to make changes and push the envelope of status quo, there will be people around you who are "stamp collecting". They do not like it when changes are made that impact them. They may not like it when you get a promotion and they did not. Just like the merchandise in the redemption store, there are any number of items of which they can choose to "collect stamps" on you.

It may take a long time for them to "collect enough stamps' to go to the redemption store; but, when they do collect enough stamps, they will do so. At that time, they want a part of you. Rather than working with you as part of the team, they start collecting, waiting for the right moment –for themselves—to redeem those stamps in any way that they can to discredit you, put you down, or to at least keep you from succeeding any further.

If these collectors have already made up their minds about you, it could already be too late. Perceptions can become reality too often, if given enough "spin" and enough pieces of information to shade the truth. Fortunately, there have been only a few times when I felt that someone wanted to redeem his/her stamps for my job, or at least have a negative impact on my reputation; but, when it did happen, it was tough to accept and sometimes difficult to overcome. It was rare that it got to a boiling point.

In my career, I have had staff members who could not put their egos aside in order to be managed or coached, if it went against their egos or opinions. They would use their stamps with certain volunteers to plant the seed of doubt or to cast a shadow on one decision or another. Sometimes the redemption ended up with the volunteers inserting themselves and turning a decision into a conflict that forces other people to choose sides or alternative actions.

It is very difficult when key volunteers, interested parties, or Board Members get in the middle of management and try to influence the situation *after* the decision has been made. If "special called meetings" occur and your decisions are the subject of the meetings, you know that there are some books of stamps that are wanting to be redeemed. I am confident that most people can identify with situations like this.

Whether it is a fellow employee, a community leader, a board member or someone else, there will probably come a time when someone has "collected stamps" on you. When that time comes, recognize it for what it is. Realize that the stamp books are present. Also, know that while they have been collecting stamps on you, you have been making a real difference for many others who *do* appreciate your efforts.

Have confidence during those trying times that your character and your strength as a leader will grow. There is no way to put a value on the input and impact that you can make for others by doing your best. That growth can never be purchased at a redemption store. Somewhere along the way of stamp collecting, you, too, will benefit and be able to cash in on the joy and realization in knowing you made a real difference.

6

A Good Name

We were a low income, poor family by today's standards. Both Mom and Dad worked fulltime. We never worried about having enough to eat or about having a roof over our heads. I thought ice milk was ice cream. Of course, it was cheaper, so that is why we bought it. All I knew was that it tasted good, no matter what they called it.

We lived in a small house with a coal heater, no air conditioner, and one bathroom with a tub and no shower. Of course, today, most families have central air and heat and several bathrooms in their homes. I'll bet most kids have never seen a piece of coal, and not taking a shower would be considered cruel and unusual punishment for most of them.

My family owned only one car at a time, and it was always a used one with many miles on the odometer. In fact, my parents have never owned a new car and probably never will.

One thing I remember when growing up was when Mom finally got one of those fancy TV antennas that could be put up outside on a telephone pole. My brother, Hal, and I had to go outside and turn it when we wanted to watch one of the only three channels that we could get on our one black and white TV.

I will never forget when Mom got an antenna that had a motor outside that would turn it automatically. I thought we were really something! Dad was not happy that Mom had "wasted money" on it when all we had to do was go outside and turn the thing on the pole; but once he saw how easily he could turn the antenna to pick up the baseball game or the Gospel Jubilee on Sunday mornings, he got over his disappointment.

We did not have a lot of material things, but we did not know it. We did not seem to lack for the things we needed; but, of course, as children, there were always things that my older brother, Hal, and I wanted that we just could not have because they were not necessities.

In my senior year of high school, when I began to seriously consider the possibility of going to college, I realized that to do so would be nothing short of a miracle. The first part of that miracle would be if I could even get into a school since my grades were only average in most subjects. The second, and biggest part, in my mind, was the cost. How in the world would we be able to afford the cost to attend a college?

My brother was a senior at Erskine College, and I had heard Mom and Dad talk about how tough it had been for them to provide the money to help keep him in school. Now, I was coming on his heels and there would be yet another several years for them to try to find a way to help their youngest go to college.

Mom finished high school, but Dad did not. He came from a family of share croppers. Getting an education was not nearly so important to his family as having bodies working in the fields on the farms, doing what had to be done to earn a living and to have a place to live. However, to their credit, they both wanted both my brother and me to get a college degree. Mom understood and appreciated it more than Dad since a couple of her brothers had graduated with degrees in education.

I was accepted at Spartanburg Junior College in Spartanburg, South Carolina. There was a part of me that was scared to death due to my lack of preparation with good study habits, and also, I had never been away from home for more than a few weeks at a time during the summers.

We loaded the car and headed to what Dad thought was a trip to the other end of the world…Spartanburg…only hours away. I had my suitcases, paper sacks, and a couple of boxes packed with everything I thought I needed for this new adventure of my life.

Mom told me that they had been able to get enough money to pay for the first semester of school. To this day, I do not know how they did it. They probably borrowed money from the bank and used what little bit of savings they had been able to put away.

We toured the dorm and met my new roommate. The campus was well kept and looked nice, but it did not take too long to have a complete tour.

Dad left to get the car, and Mom and I walked out to the circle where he would be pulling up to begin their trip back home. Standing there, she told me how proud she was of me, and she hoped that this would be a wonderful and exciting opportunity for me.

When Dad drove up, and I opened the door to let Mom in after our hugs and kisses, he made a couple of statements that I will never forget. The first one was that he and Mom had gotten up enough money to pay for my first semester, but he did not know what they were going to do for me to be able to stay on for the second semester. My stomach fell down to my feet. There I was, far from home, ready to start the biggest challenge of my life; and it was only going to last for one semester.

The second thing Dad told me became the foundation block that has driven me and molded me to become the person that I am today. He said, "Son, I am sorry that we don't have much money and can't give you any more than we have; but I want you to know that we have given you something that money can't buy…A GOOD NAME."

Little did I know of the profound impression those words would have upon my life.

A GOOD NAME…

How was a good name going to pay the tuition, not to mention room and board? How was a good name going to provide all the other things necessary to remain in college?

With that Mom told me they loved me and promised that we all would find a way to work out things.

It was pretty obvious what I had to do to stay in school. I had already received a work study loan working in the cafeteria, as well as a music scholarship, but there had to be more. So, my buddy and I got a job at a big car dealership in Spartanburg sweeping the showroom floors, dusting and washing the cars, and cleaning the offices. After that job, we would hurry back to campus to serve meals in the cafeteria.

That job lasted for only one semester, and it really did help out with necessary things, but it was not enough; so during the second semester, I got a second shift job working half of a second shift in a local textile mill. My job was doffing cloth, which meant that after the machines had woven a gigantic roll of cloth from dozens and dozens of spools, I took the roll off the machine and hauled it to another area for further processing. The work was hard, and the hours were crazy, but the money was good and desperately needed.

Playing in a rock and roll band was another way I found that became a great source of needed income. On weekends, my horn and voice were a part of a band that played for fraternity and sorority parties, along with other "gigs". Needless to say, I enjoyed that job the most of all. I made some good money, but I was also doing something that I loved to do, which involved music.

No matter what job or what situation I found myself in while attending college, I always heard my dad's words in my mind, saying that a good name was one thing that money could not buy.

I completed my Associate of Arts Degree at Spartanburg Junior college and was accepted as a junior at Erskine College in Due West, South Carolina. While at Erskine, I also had work study grants and loans. I worked in the public relations department and served as the announcer for our home basketball games, among other jobs. Changing tires, changing oil, pumping gas, wiping windshields, and doing anything else customers asked me to do was my Thursday through Saturday job at a local Gulf gas station. However, no matter what the job was, Dad's words about A GOOD NAME never left me.

After finishing Erskine in two years, I became a teacher and a coach in a Title One middle school back in my hometown of Sumter, South Carolina. Following that, I was an admissions officer at a junior college in Chesterfield, South Carolina, as well as the first men's basketball coach there. Finally, I began my career in the chamber of commerce profession where I remained for nearly 40 years.

In my 42 years of full-time work, there have been many difficult times where I found myself dealing with some very difficult situations. It would have been much easier at times if I had only given in or not stood up for what I felt was the right thing to do or what I believed in. I would not have had to go through the meetings, negotiations, and backroom politics if I had just given in and turned my head or allowed just anything with which I disagreed to be done.

As with most leaders who are in positions of trying to be change agents, your efforts and goals, while always trying to do your best, will not be appreciated by everyone. There will always be some people who can and, unfortunately, will find fault in your decisions, long after you are gone; and like any Monday Morning Quarterback, those people can certainly justify their opinions.

To the best of my abilities, I have taken the challenge of keeping A GOOD NAME to heart. I hope that my family can always be proud of the fact that their son, husband, Dad, or Granddaddy has something that money cannot buy...A GOOD NAME.

7

"Man up"---Who's Responsible?

In my former profession of running a Chamber of Commerce, the question was often asked, "What does a chamber of commerce do?" The quick answer was that we sell maps. However, the best answer was that if you have seen one chamber, then you have seen one chamber. They are all different and unique, governed by a volunteer Board of Directors.

The mission of the Chamber of Commerce in Columbus, Georgia, where I was the CEO & President was: To be the regional leader in business and community development for the Valley Partnership Region. A big part of our mission was economic development, which meant that part of our role was to assist existing businesses with their needs, as well as recruitment of new businesses, with the bottom line being retention or expansion of new jobs and new capital investment.

In the economic development world, there is no prize for finishing in second place. You might work for over a year or two recruiting a single business. You may beat out dozens of cities and states, even other countries, for this new investment; but when the dust and the dollars settle and you come in second, your city and the potential jobs that business represented were beaten, and it does not matter how close the score was. No one cares about second place because all those jobs and investments amount to nothing more than big, fat zeros on the scoreboard.

What most people do not see is that a lot of experience can be gained by coming in second. They were not kidding when they talk about the agony of defeat. Yet, it is important to dig out something positive from all the debris. A lot of energy, money, and staff time is invested into securing a project. The potential of new jobs and capital investment can be very energizing, and that excitement and enthusiasm can be very contagious among all who are involved. After all, a healthy economy can do a lot to assist many of the negative issues burdening a community or region. Most departments cost the local government money and resources; but when new growth occurs, the tide rises and everyone's boat floats higher.

Many communities are so eager, and perhaps almost desperate, for good news regarding any kind of growth that they will settle for almost anything that creates jobs. Fortunately, the Columbus region was not that desperate; but the pressure to attract quality jobs in an area of business that would be sustainable was pretty high.

At one time, our region had over 32,000 jobs in the textile industry. Today, there are less than 1,000. This is not unique to Columbus or to the South; but by design, there has been a mature and well-funded program to recruit the kinds of jobs and businesses that our region wants and needs.

We were "on the short list" of a $100,000,000 project. That meant that in this case there were only two sites left in the real competition—one in Georgia and one in Alabama. The company vying for our attention was a German-owned company producing medical products used for dialysis. For the novice, the key elements that made this such an important potential "get" for Columbus were simple – big investment, medical device manufacturer, international company that did not have a presence in the South, good paying jobs, and a very "green" business, to borrow the ecologically friendly term. This type of business was what economic development recruitment was all about.

After many months of work, we, along with the other final competitors, were invited to give our final presentation for the company. We were ready. The incentive package was very strong and the presentation was top drawer.

After our presentation on Monday, the company said they would make their final decision by noon, Thursday. Our team had until noon on Thursday if there was anything we wanted to change; but after that, it was too late.

In the economic development business, it is not unusual for deadlines to be set, then changed for no apparent reason. Many times the reasons are company related; but they are the customer, and you play by their rules whenever and however you can.

We discussed our project proposal and made positive adjustments. We were waiting on, as well as depending upon, the State to put their final proposal on the table in order to have a complete package. Since the State folks were with us during the recruitment of this project and also present during the presentations, we knew that they had some work to do to "sharpen their pencils", as well.

For two days, we kept in touch with our State partners on what they were going to present to the company as far as the State's proposal. Every day, we were told that they were working on it, but the final decision had to be made by the director with approval from then Georgia Governor Sonny Purdue. This certainly was not unusual, given the financial incentives – things like tax exemptions on equipment, free workforce training, and discounted land costs – the State was offering. Unfortunately, the director was not able to meet with the company during our Monday meeting; but his representative was there and understood the company's deadline.

On the morning of the noon deadline, we were told that the State still had not been able to get the necessary approvals of their presentation, but they were working on it. Our jaws and hearts dropped. With a $100 million investment on the line, all we knew was that they were "working on it". This was simply not acceptable.

While the company representatives were literally driving down the interstate to visit the Alabama team's proposed site, since they had not heard from the Georgia team, our state representatives called with a verbal commitment to the company. It was not good enough.

We lost the bid. The company chose a site about 35 miles away… in Alabama.

Months later, we visited the company in Germany on another recruitment trip. They shared with us the turn of events that had happened during this process. In essence, they told us that Georgia had the project… but lost it.

Perhaps you can imagine the frustration and great disappointment that ensued over the loss of such an excellent project. All I could think of was that the people of Columbus would be missing out on a state-of-the-art company in an industry that was essentially recession-proof.

After the announcement was made by the State of Alabama, there was the inevitable – somewhat heated -- conversation about why we lost; what exactly went wrong?

No matter how we tried to explain or provide insight, it all came down to the State of Georgia missing the company's deadline; and that was the bottom line. It did not matter that our team felt that our presentation was better, our proposal stronger, and our incentives more enticing; the company's decision was final.

Several months later, we had our top team of volunteers and our staff in the Governor's Office in Atlanta to ask for the state's help with a big local business expansion. When the Governor came into the room, we all stood; he thanked us for coming, and we sat down. The next part of the conversation was one way—from the Governor to us.

He began by telling about how, as parents, you try to do the very best for all of your children. You want to treat them all fairly and not do more for one than you would do for the other. After all, they were all your children. We were not sure where this was going, but it surely did not feel like a pep talk.

Then, the Governor began to explain that he was extremely disappointed in our team with the negative comments made about the medical project that was lost. He said that he did not like the comments that became publicized by the press in the aftermath; and he, frankly, was not happy with our team.

Needless to say, I think we all felt like we had been taken behind the woodshed for an old-fashioned whipping. In retrospect, perhaps the Governor was right in his expression of the public statements about what his team had not done in this case. After all, he is the governor and was elected by the people of Georgia to take care of the state's best interest. However, even with all of that being said, the bottom line was that the company told us that Georgia lost the project due to the inability to deliver a proposal within the timeframe of the project.

I waited for the Governor to finish talking before speaking up for my team. I said, "Governor, I will take full responsibility for how this happened". I explained that in our desire and drive to recruit this investment of capital and jobs, which would have been a game changer for our region, we did voice our frustration and disappointment publicly. In the heat of the battle and in the aftermath that ensued, keeping quiet was not an option that I took. I asked that he blame me for the negative press and to try to understand and forgive me for how this happened.

Governor Purdue made a few short comments, and in essence, said he hoped we had learned from this situation and that we all needed to be a part of the team in selling Georgia.

Then, we began the conversation about why we were there, which was to ask for the State's help with an existing company's expansion. The company, with corporate headquarters located in Columbus, was AFLAC. To do this, we again wanted to create a proposal that would include state and local incentives.

The Governor and his staff worked with us; and together, we put a competitive package on the table, along with our local proposal. AFLAC made a commitment that created over 2,500 jobs and over $80 million of new capital investments.

The bottom line of this story is not about the German company's decision not to locate in Georgia. It is not about what happened during the recruitment phase and the final decision process. It also is not about trying to make the State or a former Governor look bad. There is usually plenty of blame to go around when someone wants to do so.

The professional and personal lessons learned by telling this story are about ACCEPTING RESPONSIBILITY and accepting whatever the consequences, to learn from the past, and hopefully, to avoid the same results in the future.

As the leader of the professional staff, I had to man-up; I had to accept responsibility for what happened on my watch. There was no one else to blame. That is the way I am wired. It is in my DNA. I am not looking for a pat on the back because in that meeting, I showed my backside; and it got smacked.

Sometimes, despite all our best efforts, things do not work in our favor; and when our plans and aspirations go up in flames, someone is going to have to take the blame.

In my career, I have been taken behind the woodshed several times. Decisions do not always end up like they were intended. I have had heat applied because there was a lot of smoke in the kitchen, and someone needed to suffer. Retreating, or bailing out, in my opinion, is a short term fix to a longer term solution. When there is heat in the kitchen, deal with it. Sweating is okay. Finding a possible solution is the bottom line.

Rarely, have I been on the receiving end of continued persecution or retaliation once the admission of responsibility and apology were given. Of course, there are a few folks who will never forget or forgive. I truly believe that most Boards of Directors or Stockholders want honesty and no passing of the buck when issues present themselves that end up having negative impacts.

In my opinion, there are too many people in the private sector and not-for-profit worlds, as well as too many political leaders, who would rather spread the blame to others. They themselves need to man-up and take responsibility for failure.

The world is filled with those willing to send someone else to the woodshed, but few are willing to take that walk themselves. Do not be one of those people.

8

It's About Attitude

Over the years, I have given many speeches to leadership classes and to other groups; but when I am in the audience, I listen intently for words and ideas that can serve me in my own leadership role.

One of the people that I consider to be an excellent icon on leadership is Phil Tomlinson, retired CEO of TSYS, one of the world's largest credit card processing companies. TSYS is headquartered in Columbus, Georgia. Having Phil around as an active and engaged community leader was a true blessing.

Phil gave a speech that resonated particularly with me. During his presentation, Tomlinson spoke of these attributes of leadership –passion, enthusiasm, perseverance, common sense, humanity, discipline, integrity, and being a team player.

Passion: Most people do not remember what the preacher said last Sunday. They might remember a couple of key points; but they will remember if he was enthusiastic, full of energy, and humorous. Someone with passion has to share it with others. The best thing about passion is that it is contagious. A passionate person raises passion in others. We all have been there, witnessing those magical moments when passion drove a point home so honestly and directly that everyone in the audience was ready to get involved... at least temporarily.

Enthusiasm: If you could bottle it, it would outsell every energy drink on the market. I once heard someone say that real enthusiasm is being on your honeymoon, walking across the room to turn off the light, and being in bed before the room gets dark. Now, that is real enthusiasm!

Perseverance: A successful career is a marathon, not a sprint. Many people want the title, the compensation, and other benefits that come with being at the top of the company; but most fall short when it comes to understanding what it takes to not only get there, but also what it takes to stay there.

Common Sense: It is important to focus on reality, not just dreams and aspirations. We all know people in the public and private sectors who see the world as they would like for it to be, rather than see it as it is. If it does not make good common sense, it probably should not be done.

Humility: Phil said not to take yourself too seriously. He also said not to worry about who gets the credit because what happens is amazing if you do not care who gets the credit. Remember that people do not care how much you know until they know how much you care.

Discipline: It takes professional and personal discipline to be an effective leader. A leader must control his/her emotions and respond with a rational and proper decision for the right reasons.

Integrity: The ethics of a leader matter. Honesty is still always the best policy, whether it be in business or in personal matters.

Listening to Phil's talk, it is no wonder that under his leadership, TSYS has become a world leader in their business. Many companies have gained great market shares by practicing good leadership skills, both short and long term.

When I first moved to Georgia, someone gave me tickets to see an Atlanta Braves game. The Braves had been awful for a long time, but this year they had a chance to go to the playoffs. We were in the upper decks, but we were there, nonetheless. I have never chopped so much in my life; but for eight straight innings, we chopped enthusiastically.

In the 9th inning of the seventh, and also, the deciding game of the National Championships, Sid Bream was on second base. The announcers liked to joke that he moved with the speed of a glacier, and they were not kidding. From where we were sitting, it was hard to see if he was moving at all. Francisco Cabrera was hitting. I had never heard of him and surely did not know anything about his hitting, but we were standing up and chopping, like lifelong Braves fans.

If you are a Braves fan, you know how it ended. Cabrera got a hit. Bream went "streaking" home and was called safe as he slid in to the plate. BRAVES WIN! BRAVES WIN! BRAVES WIN!

We were jumping up and down, giving high fives to anyone we could reach and yelling, "WE WON!" "WE WON!" It was quite a reversal, considering that only a few years before, the likely chant would have been something along the lines of, "They can't beat a high school team."

I do not know if the chopping helped, but it surely did not hurt. There were not many people that night in the Braves stadium who did not think the Braves were going to win, even with two outs and Sid Bream on second. The enthusiasm was electric. It was real, and it made a difference.

Whether it is a baseball team, a cheerleading squad, or a team of employees, most people want to be around winners. When there is a *losing* environment, you often hear the word "they". *They* can't; *they* won't, *they* couldn't. However, when there is a *winning* attitude, a positive environment, you hear "we" most of the time. *We* can; *we* will, and *we* did.

Sometimes, that extra ingredient, like enthusiasm, is enough to push what might be a negative situation into a positive one. In spite of the past or the near-present, with the right amount of enthusiasm, anything can happen. The right amount of enthusiasm can make a real difference.

Do not listen to what "they" say because "they" do not always know what your team can do. Instead, listen when someone talks about "we". Then, listen carefully. "We" can figure this out. "We" have got to find a way to make this happen.

One of my closest friends is Neil Stillwell. Neil says that he is a genuine "redneck" from Phenix City, Alabama and is proud of it. Calling the name of the city PC is about as close as he will ever get to using the letters PC (politically correct). Neil says what he means and means what he says. His stories can make you laugh and make you cry because they are genuine and come from his heart and soul.

Neil began his career in the sporting goods business with NEIL'S SPORTING GOODS in Columbus, GA. He gave away a free T-shirt when the customer bought a pair of shoes. He called that customer a walking billboard. Long before the big companies started pouring money into endorsements for athletes and coaches to wear their hats, shoes, jerseys, etc., Neil was the pioneer of endorsements.

Coach Pat Dye of Auburn University asked Neil if he would like to go to Auburn to sell some hats at a football game. Being a super salesman, Neil jumped at the chance and sold out of hats in the first couple of hours. Every week, the sales got bigger and bigger until Neil decided to take it a big step further. He worked out a deal to provide free hats to the coaches and team, as well as providing some financial incentives to the head coach. If the coach wore "The GAME" hat during the game, Neil paid him. If the game was televised, he paid more. If it were a bowl game, he paid even more than that. Well, word got around about the hat deal and pretty soon Neil was getting phone calls from many South Eastern Conference (SEC) coaches, as well as most of the major universities and colleges in America about a similar deal. He says that he figured they thought 'this ole redneck' from Alabama didn't know what he was doing by paying them to wear his free hats. Of course, Neil was laughing all the way to the bank by making the deals.

In his "good ole boy" way, Neil told folks that he was buying hats for $3 and selling them for $15; and he thought that the 12% profit was good enough. Of course, when folks heard him say that, some wondered if he was kidding or if he really knew what he was doing. He knew exactly what he was doing!

The sporting goods business grew into a business called The Game. That business became very successful and was later sold to Russell Athletics for $43 million. Neil then started a new company named KUDZU, which became a very successful company, as one of the top companies selling to NASCAR, almost all major colleges and universities, Bass Pro, the Kentucky Derby, and PGA Golf Tournaments, as well as many top retailers and businesses. When the bottom fell out of the licensed products industry five years later, they bought back the assets from Russell for only $3.8 million. Even using "Neil's math", that's an unbelievable business deal!

The Game bought the exclusive rights for marketing, sales, and distribution for a company known as SALT LIFE. Jeff Stillwell, Neil's son, is the President of SALT LIFE.

Neil and Jeff's story is a perfect example of the phrase about an apple not falling far from the tree. Jeff is taking SALT LIFE to unbelievable growth, building on the foundation from the past successes of Neil's Sporting Goods, The Game, and KUDZU. Neil is as proud as he can be of his son, as well as his son of his dad.

Neil is a most humble man with lots of colorful stories about business, fishing, and his family; but he is quick to tell you of the time in the early days when, after another 80 hour week, he counted up the profits for the day, and it was only 42 cents! In his little office, when it appeared that the business might not make it, he prayed a prayer to God and asked Him to help him not to fail. He promised to always put God first, his family second, and then his business. It was at that point and time in his business and personal life that his attitude became solidified…somehow, someway, with God as his helper, he would be successful.

Thinking about Neil reminds me of a statement that I have used often in some of my presentations:

WHEN YOU CHANGE YOUR THINKING, YOU CHANGE YOUR BELIEFS;

WHEN YOU CHANGE YOUR BELIEFS, YOU CHANGE YOUR EXPECTATIONS;

WHEN YOU CHANGE YOUR EXPECTATIONS; YOU CHANGE YOUR ATTITUDE'

WHEN YOU CHANGE YOUR ATTITUDE, YOU CHANGE YOUR BEHAVIOR;

WHEN YOU CHANGE YOUR BEHAVIOR, YOU CHANGE YOUR PERFORMANCE;

WHEN YOU CHANGE YOUR PERFORMANCE, YOU CHANGE YOUR LIFE.

Life is full of challenges and opportunities. As long as we live, there will be things that come our way, both professionally and personally, that can impact our attitudes, if we let them. I believe the biggest challenge we face is the person we see in the mirror. We can always find someone who would trade places with us in a moment if he/she could.

9

The Smartest Person in the Room

We have all been in their presence…the Smartest Person in the Room. At least they think they are the Smartest Person in the Room. They are the folks with all the answers. They may have just been elected or hired, but they already know more about what you should or should not do than anyone else.

I am a fairly simple man. I often found out that I did not even know the question, much less the answer. The longer I was in management, the more I realized this truth.

In Columbus, a way of thinking was developed that, I believe, became a movement of sorts. It was born out of a vision from one of our community's greatest visionaries, Mr. Bill Turner, Past Chairman and CEO of the W.C. Bradley Co. The movement was known as the Servant Leadership Program; and in addition to gaining regional and national attention, it also became a program at Columbus State University, as well as at other universities. It is a four-year program focused on learning to share power, helping people develop and perform as highly as possible, and putting the needs of others first. Serving others is nothing new; but in these days, it seems that people are more concerned about themselves than anyone else.

Mr. Turner told this story of one Halloween. A kindergarten class from the St. Luke School in Columbus made its customary visit to the corporate office. The students, wearing costumes, were excited to get Halloween candy from the various offices.

Given the chance, some children will grab as much candy as their tiny little hands can hold. Well, Mr. Turner was running low on candy, and he said he was having to keep a close eye on some of the children to keep them from getting more than their fair share, fearing he would run out of candy.

That is when he met Little Miss Tinkerbell.

She was as cute as she could be. She looked into his basket and noticed that he was running low on candy. Then, she looked into her own basket; and without hesitation, took some of her own candy and put it into Mr. Turner's basket.

Obviously, this little girl had just exhibited the purest form of Servant Leadership by giving some of her candy to someone else, just because she could and because she wanted to share.

Can you imagine what would happen if more people understood and practiced this way of thinking and living? In my opinion and probably that of many, Mr. Bill Turner is one of the smartest people I have ever met. He does not have to tell you he is smart; instead, he lets his heart guide his words, his soul, and his actions.

There are many past, present, and future leaders who owe a great deal to the quiet, steady leader, Mr. Bill...one of the least boastful and most humble people that I have ever known.

In my career, I have been in many meetings where the person with the biggest title, as far as rank or organizational structure, drove the outcome. When the meetings were over, I was often left wondering why anyone else bothered to show up when that Smartest Person in the Room already had all the answers. Apparently, he/she needed an audience to witness the outcome.

However, I have also been in meetings without the Smartest Person in the Room. Even though it became apparent who had the most knowledge, everyone was encouraged to participate, to share thoughts, options, and ideas. Those meetings were easier in which to get people eager to come and participate, since everyone felt as though they were on equal ground and were being heard.

Once, I was in a meeting that was coming to an end, when an employee took advantage of those in attendance to try to get another issue on the table to be resolved. While it could have been ignored or put it off until another time, the leaders instead addressed the employee's concerns and resolved the issue, then and there. It was a great use of time and situation by the employee, and he got the job done.

Later that day, an email made the rounds stating that putting a new item on the table without it first being added to the agenda was totally unacceptable. Granted, there was merit to following protocol; but instead of praise and thanks, there was "hand slapping". Initiative was exhibited but rewarded with negative feedback.

Allowing your staff room to solve a problem by using their own initiatives brings about positive impact. They should not have to follow a long chain of command, but rather be able to trust the responsible party with hearing their concerns without fear of reprisals.

In this case, I do not think it was about style. It was about making sure that nothing was said that might reflect in any way upon the Smartest Person in the Room, who expected everything to begin at the top and end there, as well.

I read a book about a platoon during the Vietnam War that suffered fewer injuries and casualties than many others. The men succeeded because every member of the unit was treated equally. They shared everything. Rank was never a barrier. All the unit was allowed, even encouraged, to share what they believed worked and what did not work with each mission.

The leader recognized that the success of the mission depended upon the whole team giving input and guidance of lessons learned, as well as things to consider for the next mission. By allowing and encouraging everyone to participate, the whole unit was successful.

Most of us have encountered leaders who were not interested in hearing the ideas of others. Generally, any success they had was short lived because they could not get everyone on board.

It is possible to be the Smartest Person in the Room without ever having to say it.

10

The Only One There

Too tired or too frustrated to go "that extra mile"…AGAIN. We have all been there. What I have learned during those journeys of trial and exhaustion is that one person can impact others. One person can make a difference.

That is a lesson Pat Seymour burned into my heart and soul.

At first glance, one would never know what dynamite was inside that tiny frame. Pat Seymour from Mentone, Alabama was a spunky, feisty fireball. She stood under five feet tall, often wearing something that might have been fashionable 20 years earlier; but that was part of her "packaging". She had a PhD and was one of the first women in a nationally known speaker's bureau.

Hearing the endless list of the articles and academic achievements she had been awarded could put you to sleep, and such a boring intro seemed fitting for what could only be an equally snooze-inducing lecture from some distant academic perspective. However, Pat was anything but boring. She often began by saying that she had forgotten to put on a piece of her underwear…just to make sure everyone was paying attention. From that point on, she had her audience where she wanted it…intently listening to every word.

Pat was Paul "Bear" Bryant's secret weapon. If there was a high school player that the legendary University of Alabama coach wanted to play for him, but the kid's mom was not completely sold on his playing for the University, Pat would be called in by Coach Bryant.

Pat would talk, woman-to-woman, with the young man's mother about how her baby boy would be given special attention – and tough love if necessary—to make sure he behaved.

Pat told great stories. She had a gift of timing, making her audience feel like they were right there in the middle of the story as it unfolded, watching, as it all played out.

One of her favorite stories was about the time she was selected to be the first woman in the National Speakers Association. She was proud of being a pioneer, so she called her elderly mother to share the news. After hearing the news, her mom paused before asking Pat if she was still coming for a visit so they could go to church on Sunday like she had promised.

Here is Pat thinking, "Mom, I just received this unbelievable recognition; but instead of being around folks in Tuscaloosa, Alabama, who would probably have a big reception in my honor, I am going to be in a Sunday School class listening to a bunch of old women talk about their medical problems and the next doctor's appointments." However, like a good daughter, Pat skipped the party and the accolades to be with her mother.

Unfortunately, the senior pastor was out that Sunday; and in his place was the young associate pastor. While on his way to deliver the announcements, he turned over the water glass and Pat's annoyance continued, as she is still thinking about all the things she could be doing instead of being there.

When it was time for the sermon, Pat was about ready to explode. After all, she was a nationally recognized speaker; and she, if anyone, should be delivering a memorable speech to the captive audience. However, as the young minister began his sermon, the words became so powerful that Pat would never be able to get them out of her mind.

The minister told his congregation that he did not really have a sermon prepared for that day, to which Pat silently thanked God for one answered prayer, assuming that meant the service would be blessedly short.

The young minister said that on the night before, while visiting one of the church members in the hospital, a nurse ran up to him in a panic saying that a patient was brought in after a horrible accident and was likely to die.

When he entered the room, the preacher was confronted by a person covered in blood, a person who was obviously not long for this world. He grabbed the stranger's hand and began to pray. The man in the bed began to mumble something quietly. The minister bent over the patient to better understand what the dying man was saying. He heard the words, "Preacher, I heard you preach once." Those were his last words.

It was the first death the young man had witnessed since becoming a minister. It was an experience he would never forget, an experience that left him feeling emotionally and physically drained.

The young preacher stopped by the nurse's station for something to settle his stomach, and the nurse gave him some ginger ale. After his nerves settled, he asked the nurse how many ministers had visiting privileges at the hospital. There were 250 ministers on the register. The young preacher was the only minister in the hospital.

He gathered himself and walked out to the car. Leaning against the driver's side door, the dead man's words echoed through his mind. "I heard you preach once."

Which sermon did he hear? Was it a good one? Or was it one, much like the one he was delivering on this particular Sunday, when he was not prepared? The preacher was filled with worry and regret, fearing that the stranger, whose life he had watched slip away, was now dead; and his place in eternity may very well have been key to the choices he made while he was living.

There was not a dry eye in the crowd as Pat retold this story. That is when she set the hook.

"Ladies and gentlemen," she said, "every day we meet people; we come in contact with strangers and friends. We may only meet them once, so can we afford to take the easy way out or to do our best?"

I am often reminded of Pat and this, as well as other stories she told, particularly when I am preparing for a keynote speech. I think about the words of a dying man. What if I hear someone say, "I heard you speak at a conference"? What impact did I make on them? Was it a speech for which I was prepared; was it one in which I did my best; or was I just going through the motions?

Few of us will save a life or help determine where someone will spend eternity; but we can all plant seeds of encouragement that can grow into important foundation blocks for living. Which one will they hear? Which one will they see? Hopefully, it will be our best.

We may be the only person who had an opportunity at that special time in their life to be there for them. It may be a speech, a phone call, or an email to someone, but giving it your best can be impactful and encouraging. It just might make a difference in someone's life.

11

May I Be Honest With You?

"May I be honest with you?"

Every time I hear whose words, I automatically think, "Well, were you being dishonest with me before?" At least, that is what seems to be implied, as though everything said before were not totally true. Rarely does anything positive follow such a leading question.

We all know what they really mean, or do we? In these days, we are so conditioned to be politically correct and sensitive to the feeling of others, I often worry that honesty has become a thing of the past.

When I used to interview someone for a job, one of the questions I asked right in the middle of the conversation was, "Do you believe there should be degrees of honesty in a work environment?" The responses I often heard were amazing. Too often, the response was, "Yes"; or "Well, you don't have to tell the whole truth."

When I questioned further, some responses came back along the lines of, "Well, everybody does it to some degree." Or, "As long as it doesn't hurt anyone's feelings", was another response.

Maybe I am "old school", but I believe you are either honest or dishonest. Telling parts or pieces of the truth is dishonest. There is no middle ground, no in between when it comes to the truth. If someone fudges on little things; then, what is the gauge they use to determine when the whole truth is needed, or is not needed? Of course, common sense should be used, rather than acting like the bull in the china shop when responding to a question.

I recall asking an employee if a project on which we were working was completed and ready to go. The employee responded that it was ready; so, I told the key volunteer, who was chairing the project, that it was ready. Then, I found out a little while later that it was *about* ready to go, or *would be* ready to go…at least as far as the employee was concerned.

At that point, we had a credibility issue beyond just a project implementation issue. I immediately wondered how many other times I had been given the answer I *wanted* to hear instead of the truth. By that point, we were in damage control mode, meaning there were extra work and energy needed to get the project completed on time.

In my 38 years of working with volunteers, SELDOM did they "rip my lips off" for making a mistake or missing a deadline. Yes, there were times of difficulty, but each mistake had learning opportunities. Some volunteers were more professional than others, for sure; but few of them were out for blood if the mistake was explained up front, with details of how it could be fixed or modified.

There were times when a staff member shared some bad news on a project that was messed up, or when an error in judgement occurred. It was then that I always tried to remember to respond like those really super volunteers had done…Listen, ask questions, and see if there might be a learning opportunity with it, after the damage control had been developed.

We know there are a few people who will never be professional in how they respond to an issue. We also know that it may not be politically correct to tell the truth. However, I have found that in the long run, the truth is always better than whatever *part* of the truth may be used. Yet, all around us are examples of how people will tell a partial truth in hopes that part of the truth is good enough.

Do any of these phrases sound familiar? "I didn't have sex with that woman." "If you like your doctor, you can keep you doctor."

Those words were not the total truth, but they bought the speakers some time and deflected a lot of negativity; but, you know, telling partial truths has been around as long as mankind has been on Earth. Remember the Garden of Eden? Adam and Eve had everything they needed, but they wanted more; so they went out and took what they wanted. When they were caught, they were desperate for excuses. Adam even blamed Eve. Eve blamed the serpent; and, so it has continued until today, when telling lies and partial truths can be justified or explained away. We now hear words like, "I misspoke" or "I misremembered". The Good Book says that the truth will set you free...I'm all for that!

Sometimes honesty comes with a price. Generals have lost their commands by telling the truth on the progress of war and its probable outcome. Sometimes, those in ultimate authority do not want to hear the truth and are more likely to blame the truth teller than to fairly assess the situation.

There is scripture about people having "itchy ears", meaning that telling people what they want to hear will then make it easier for you to get what you want. The promise of Social Security is another good example. Does anyone reading this book believe that we can continue to borrow from the fund and still be able to pay the amounts to those who have earned Social Security at the present rate? Yet, if an elected official were to make a campaign on telling the whole truth about Social Security and what must be done to fix it, they would probably never get elected.

Perhaps our courts had it right when commanding those taking the witness stand to tell the truth, the whole truth, and nothing but the truth because there is no middle ground when it comes to telling the truth. Too bad there is not a buzzer that goes off every time that did not happen.

Honesty is always the best policy. Usually, dishonesty brings on additional actions or words, which then create more static and more issues, which further impact the situation.

I read a story about four sophomores who were about to take a final exam. They were confident that they would be able to make a good grade; so, on the weekend before finals, they went to visit some friends and had a big party weekend. They slept all day on Sunday. They did not make it back to the university in time for the final exam. Instead, they spent some time studying and went as a group to the professor explaining that they had been out of town and had had a flat tire that caused them to miss the time for the final exam.

The professor decided to give them the exam the next day. That night they studied and studied and were relieved to have been given this extra time. The next day, the professor put the students in separate rooms to take the exam. After answering the first question, they all thought that it was going to be a real breeze. When they each turned to the second page, they read the following words, "For 95 points: which tire?"

The students thought that they had the system to win; but the professor had the honor to beat their system.

I have often thought about the real lessons learned by the students from the professor. They, hopefully, learned a life-long lesson, well-worth more than a grade on an exam. The outcome would have been much different IF they had been honest from the beginning.

12

But, I Have a Plan

Every successful business or organization knows that having a solid, well-vetted plan is essential for success. Of course, selling that plan takes a vision, a way of explaining why this plan needs to be developed, and the differences it can make. Without a good vision, the greatest of plans can fall on deaf ears, or not be successful.

A sound plan is a key ingredient, but it has to be sold as part of the vision. A couple of good dictionary definitions for vision are: a vivid mental image; the ability to see; the perceptual experience of seeing.

The Bible refers to the necessity of having vision in Proverbs 29:18, which states, "Without a vision, the people perish." A strong vision can transform organizations, companies, cities, and communities. There is a big difference in a vision and a catchy phrase. Unless the vision is bold and exciting, and can capture the imagination of those impacted, it can be a hard sell.

When I moved to Columbus, Georgia in 1988, the community had what I like to call an Eeyore mentality, after the perpetually gloomy donkey from *Winnie the Pooh*. Like many communities and organizations, people around Columbus fell back on phrases familiar to the put-upon, "We tried that once", or "unless 'they' approve it, it will never happen". Another phrase used a lot was, "You're not from here, are you?" Such perceptions are easily validated. When you expect to lose, you usually will do so.

Columbus was mostly a textile mill town and a military town. When I first got to Columbus, there were about 30,000 people working in the textile mills. Today, there are less than 1,000! Thank goodness for those jobs and their impact on the economy.

Talking about diversity in business was not something some business leaders wanted to do, but there were whispers about the necessity of change being discussed in some circles. Diversification is what makes a company – or in this case a town—sustainable. By slowly diversifying, the economy began to gain traction in the right circles. However, there was something else even less popular among those in charge. It was community development – or Quality of Life.

The Chattahoochee River runs through Columbus, connecting the states of Georgia and Alabama. When I first moved to Columbus, one of the only reasons anyone went down to the river was to do a little fishing.

"The Hooch", as locals call it, was once the major energy source for over 20 textile mills, with the water from the river being used to run the turbines in the mills. The river was the literal lifeblood of the textile community. However, those days are long gone. The only things left of the river's industrial past are a few vacant textile mills and an old power house where two turbines were housed.

In 1988-89, a small group of Columbus volunteers decided to visit several communities that, like Columbus, had a river running through or near them. After the volunteers visited some similar communities, they came back home overflowing with ideas to be considered so that "The Hooch" could be reclaimed as a source of pride and economic possibilities.

"Creative theft" is a good way to think about it. Seeing what others have done – both successfully and unsuccessfully—can go a long way toward completing a vision. Many businesses have learned from those who have come before, seeing what was successful and adapting it to their own businesses. Our group wanted to hire an architectural firm to commit some of their ideas to paper, based on possibilities in terms of public space and utilization.

Once all that was done, a public meeting was held presenting the vision-- or perhaps dreams, as some might say—or outright hallucinations, according to others—we had for what could be done with The Hooch. Many of the ideas made sense; and the general opinion was along the lines of, "Well...why haven't we done that already?" There were many items that pushed the imagination; but we had a vision, and that vision required some bold steps.

At that time, Columbus, like many other cities, was struggling with a tremendously challenging environmental issue—Combined Sewer Overflow (CSO). CSO is where the sanitary sewer and the storm water sewer ran together. During big rains, it created quite a mess when the city's raw sewage overflowed into the river.

Unfortunately, most of our city's CSO issues were in downtown Columbus. Trying to fix that kind of mammoth problem without completely shutting down every business and government service would be almost impossible to overcome. Thankfully, the President of the Columbus Water Works, Mr. Billy Turner, saw the presentation and the "light turned on". Instead of digging up all of downtown, Billy suggested putting a large collection pipe on the bank of the river. Once the riverbank was stabilized, a maintenance road would be built to create access to the pipe.

There were many meetings, lots of plans developed, and millions of dollars were spent to turn this vision into a reality, curing an environmental-disaster-in-the-making at the same time. During this time, the city had an opportunity to have a vote from the citizens known as Special Purpose Local Option Sales Tax (SPLOST). If the citizens voted for the one cent sales tax, then a big part of the initial cost could be paid by the sales tax and not have it all be applied to the sewer rates of everyone.

This was an extremely complex project that took years to solidify. There were hundreds and hundreds of people who worked on it.

It became one of our community's best examples of the public and private sectors working together for the common good.

The SPLOST passed, as did the idea for fixing the CSO. A large collection pipe was put on the bank of The Hooch. The bank was stabilized, and access was made available.

What began as a vision for the river became The River Walk, in reality, one of Columbus' crowning achievements and a jewel in that elusive concept known as Quality of Life. The River Walk was featured on the cover of Georgia's official map. Thousands of folks every week are running, walking, pushing baby carriages, or biking on what is really the covering for the sewer pipe.

However, the story does not end there. Nothing breeds success like success.

We had rediscovered The Hooch by bringing a vision to life, but that was just the beginning. What was once forsaken land had become a focal point of economic growth and community potential.

The leaders of the W.C. Bradley Company, who have one of the most visionary leaders that I have ever met, Mr. Bill Turner (not related to Billy Turner who designed the CSO), also were part of the vision for the river area by providing more than just empty promises, wishful thinking, and lip service. The W.C. Bradley Company purchased some of the abandoned textiles mills, renovated them, and turned them into condos and first-class apartments. Mat Swift and his team became the real estate leader making the old mills become alive again.

Another one of their leaders, Mr. John Turner, caught the vision and expanded it to include the possibility of whitewater sports. John was the champion, along with many other public and private sector organizations. Thanks to their efforts, Columbus has the longest urban whitewater course in the world! In fact, during 2014, *USA Today* featured the course as one of the best 12 manmade adventures in the world!

Now kayaks, rafts, and thousands of whitewater and nature enthusiasts can be seen on The Hooch, appreciating today, what was just an idea or a vision, a little over a dozen years ago.

What made the difference? The river had been there long before Columbus was a city; and during the city's lifespan, it had served many roles—both vital and recreational—yet no one could have imagined what it would become; at least no one, until some community leaders, seeking a way to improve the area's quality of life, shared a vision of what might be.

Every community has potential. Of course, few have the good fortune to have a beautiful river running through its downtown; but without a vision, without a plan, without leadership and hard work, as well as a community willing to buy into that vision by supporting initiatives to bring it to life, potential alone does not amount to much.

WITHOUT A VISION, THE COMMUNITY PERISHES… THE BUSINESS FAILS…THE COUNTRY CAN BECOME DIVIDED. WITHOUT A VISION, POTENTIAL STAYS POTENTIAL INSTEAD OF BECOMING REALITY.

13

It Takes All Kinds

Thank goodness, we are uniquely different in so many ways. God has a wonderful sense of humor. If you do not think so, just watch us human beings—the way we look, talk, walk, and act--- and you will have no doubt about God's sense of humor. There are plenty of folks with whom I would be more than happy to never have to spend another minute alone, or in a crowd, for that matter. I am sure you know some of these people, or at least some just like them. However, even these folks can bring something to the table; their perspective or their opinion, as warped and misinformed as they seem at the time, can still provide some insights; although I doubt it is in any way like they imagine.

NIMBY People…

One particular group with which I have had a fair amount of dealings is the NIMBY group (NOT IN MY BACKYARD People). Undoubtedly, you have heard of them. They are the people who complain about some civic ordinance and its value…right up to the point where those in leadership try to figure out where to put such valuable necessities, such as jails, rehab centers, and landfills. These "necessities" often get the NIMBY crowd riled up. Sure they want these things; they just want them to be built *somewhere else*, like in someone else's neighborhood…*anywhere else*… as long as it is not too close to them.

Most folks want a good restaurant close by; but when the rezoning starts to take place in our neighborhood, we decide that we do not want it here, but there....in someone else's backyard.

Even though we have made some progress in disposing of our domestic trash and garbage, until we make the decision and the investment of some type of thermally treated waste disposal, we will always have the need for landfills. Do you want a landfill in your neighborhood? Probably not, but whose neighborhood do you think does want one? Our problem is that we want, or need, the benefit of these things; but we do not want to be the ones to experience the negative impacts that they may bring.

Then, comes the next group of folks. I call them the CAVE People (Citizens Against Virtually Everything). These are the folks who, no matter how much you explain, listen to, or try to find common ground with, they simply will not budge on their opinions, which, in case you were wondering is generally...NO!

CAVE People...

They just come wired that way. Whatever it is, whatever sense it may make to everyone else in the room, they do not trust, or even want to consider, any opinion, other than their own. I have tried many different ways to convince, persuade, or impact CAVE People, only to come away with frustration or major headaches.

The next group of folks are first cousins to the CAVE People. I call them the NOPE People (Not On Planet Earth). If you think the CAVE People are frustrating and difficult with which to communicate, then try your hand with the NOPE folks.

NOPE People...

The NOPE People have no interest at all in even hearing any rationale or reasons as to why something might be worth talking about. If it were left up to NOPE People, we would all be back in caves or wherever we came from, rolling stones around. Their minds are made up, and it really does not matter what you say or do to show another side or even a piece of another way to look at something. NOPE!

Not only will you get a massive headache working with these folks, but you might even experience some bumps and bruises if you are not careful. There were many experiences that I had in my career in dealing with the NOPE folks, but one comes to mind as if it happened yesterday.

One of the major missions of the Columbus Chamber of Commerce was to lead economic development in our region. Of course, having land that was suitable for building and development was the first priority for this growth potential. Our city had a landfill that was nearing the end of its usefulness. We had Jimmy Yancey, who was President of CB&T, the largest bank in town, to serve as our volunteer champion.

After many months of poring over maps and having seemingly endless conversations, we found a large piece of property that had only one owner. Utilities could be delivered to the site. The one owner happened to be the U.S. Federal Government, and the name was Fort Benning.

The 1,800 acres of land would be the largest development that our county had ever used for economic development. There were many positive aspects, other than just the land for development. The military base wanted to close its landfill, while the city of Columbus was in the process of expanding its current landfill. It felt like a real win-win situation. I always felt that it was worth the effort to make it happen any time both parties could end up winning or getting a major part of what they wanted out of a deal.

We assumed it could be somewhat controversial. Landfills and where to locate them almost always are. We also needed to make sure that other land owners did not get too anxious and start pushing up the price of land artificially.

So, we created the NFL (Need For Land) Project. Looking back, it might not have been the best acronym because a few folks thought we trying to bring a pro football team to town. Nevertheless, the NFL Project became the foundation of our efforts.

Much of this land to be involved in the swap, was in another county. There was a hearing to decide on the plan. We just knew that it would be good for that county because it meant there would be new jobs locating there.

We did not go blindly into the meeting. We expected concerns from some of the citizens and figured that, given the chance to hear our plan and the benefit it would serve to the county, eventually even those worried about the swap would come around. Simply put, the idea just made sense...for everyone.

As soon as we got near the door leading into the meeting, we heard the crowd. There were sheriff's deputies in the hall to let us into the room. It did not take long to realize that this was not a friendly crowd. Before the meeting officially began, a woman seated in the jury box stood up and threw a hangman's noose over the banister. She wanted us to know that was how she felt about the land swap.

Needless to say, it all went downhill from there. We did our best to explain what we were doing, and why. We heard their concerns about taking their land off the tax rolls, which was a legitimate concern, and said we would work with them to find a way to lessen the impact, which we did; but after nearly an hour of one person after another telling us in no uncertain terms exactly why they did not want the land swap and why they would not support it, finding the nearest exit became our main goal.

A U.S. Congressman, Richard Ray, got very involved. Due to his intervention, restrictions were written and passed that mandated that no county could purchase property in another county without a formal process being followed. In retrospect, it was not such a bad outcome; but at the time, it felt like just another obstacle to be overcome. All told, it took 13 years for this win-win idea to become a reality.

The rest of the story is now history. We swapped land with another land owner in another part of the region, which brought a new business into that county. The NFL became Muscogee Technology Park and is one of the finest in the South. It already has five businesses in the park with Blue Cross Blue Shield building a campus that will have around 2,000 employees.

While the journey is not over, it was well worth all the headaches, arguments, and worry about potential bodily harm at the hands of the NOPE, CAVE, and NIMBY people. There are people who are gainfully employed, and the local governments have been able to expand their tax bases, providing more revenue.

The NOPE folks had a right to speak out and let their voices be heard…but in the end, the win-win idea became just that.

14

She Was an Angel, but I Wasn't

You know you are a pretty good prankster when your maid is praying for you and locking you out of the house.

My family lived in the small town of Sumter, South Carolina, which was about 45 miles from the capital, Columbia. Sumter was known for three things—Swan Lake, Shaw Air Force Base, and furniture mills.

Before Dad became a full-time minister, he worked for Sumter Concrete Company, while Mom worked in the office of one of the furniture plants. They were both hard working folks who never took a sick day off and were thankful to give a good day's work for a good day's pay.

When my parents were at work, my older brother, Hal, and I were blessed to have a wonderful saint of a woman who came to the house every day to work. Her name was Dorothy. She did not drive, so for many years Mom picked her up in the mornings and took her back home in the afternoons when she finished work. In those days, we called Dorothy our maid; but these days, she would be known as our housekeeper. All Hal and I knew was that she was a sweet, God-fearing woman who was there taking care of the chores every afternoon when we got home from school.

We loved Dorothy, and she loved us. At times, she needed every ounce of that love to put up with my childish pranks. Years later, when I had grown out of my shenanigans—mostly—I visited

Dorothy. She was old, and her health was failing; but that did not keep her from laughing about old times back when "Mr. Mike", as she always called me, could find nothing more fun to do than scaring the living daylights out of her.

One day, Hal was going to bring his college roommate home for the weekend. I could not avoid the temptation of making his visit memorable. Before they got there, I told Dorothy that Hal's friend had "fits" sometimes. The way to keep him from swallowing his tongue when he fell down on the floor with one of those "fits" was to put a spoon under his tongue. Dorothy could not believe that "Mr. Hal" would bring home somebody who had "fits". Now, she had one more thing to worry about in addition to her housework. I told her that I would help her, as I promptly got a big spoon and put it on the kitchen counter to remind her of what to do if this boy had one of his "fits".

Everything was fine when they first arrived. We introduced Hal's friend to Dorothy, who gave him something to eat before they went to Hal's room. While they were gone, I kept reminding Dorothy about his "fits" and telling her that I sure hoped he did not have one while he was at our house. I knew it was getting to her because each time I mentioned "fits", Dorothy would mumble her favorite phrase—a prayer really-- one I heard often, "Lord Jesus, help me."

Hal and his roommate came back into the den. Little did I know that the guy had allergies that came with a frequent cough. When the first cough came, I was standing by Dorothy and snatched up the spoon, ready to hand it to her. Nothing happened other than the cough, but I knew Dorothy was on alert and ready to do what she had to do, with Jesus as her helper.

For a couple of hours, we talked; and Hal and the guy watched TV. Each time he coughed, Dorothy looked at him with those big, sweet eyes of hers to see if he was about to have a "fit". As the day ended and Mom came to take Dorothy home, there had been no incidents.

As usual, after Mom got back from taking Dorothy home, she had some questions for us. Dorothy had told Mom that her prayers had been answered that day. When Mom asked for more details, Dorothy told her all about the college boy that Hal brought home, his "fits", and her praying that that boy would not have any "fits" while she was there. It did not take long for Mom to realize what was going on; and the more suspicious Mom was about the afternoon, the more Dorothy started to suspect she might have been the victim of a "Mike prank".

When Mom got home from work the next day, we cleared up the situation with Dorothy standing there. She said that she should have known that I had made up something like that prank and said that she was just going to have to pray for me even more.

Another time, Dorothy locked me out of the house because I scared her so badly. I don't know where it came from or how it came into my possession, but I had a big ol' rubber snake. One afternoon, Dorothy was washing laundry and knowing she would hang the clothes on the clothes line, since we did not have a clothes dryer, I began forming my plan. I took the snake and placed it in the grass beside one of the clothesline poles.

When Dorothy was ready to take the clothes out to hang them on the line, I told her that I would help her. She was a little taken aback but said that she appreciated my help and that sometimes I could really be a sweet boy. Little did she know!

It was my job to hand Dorothy the clothes out of the basket, and she would pin them on the line. After about 5 minutes, I yelled… "Dorothy, don't move!" I went over to the mop that was hanging on the end of the clothesline and took it and hit down in the grass. As I did, the rubber snake came bouncing up out of the grass. Then, I hit it again, and it bounced again!

Dorothy hated snakes, and she took off running towards the house. I again heard her favorite words (at least around me), "Lord Jesus, help me!" It probably did not help that I draped the snake on the mop handle so that it looked like a really big snake that I had killed.

As I started toward the house with the "dead" snake, I told Dorothy that I had killed it, and I wanted her to see that it was dead. I heard the door lock; so I spent the rest of the afternoon, which was probably about an hour, until Mom got home, sitting outside, waiting…

When Mom got ready to take Dorothy home, I was brought into the house to tell Dorothy that I was sorry…even though I was not. In fact, the whole thing worked out just like I had planned; but I was sorry that I had been locked out of the house.

Looking back on those times, I have nothing but pleasant thoughts. Dorothy helped raise me. She loved me in spite of myself. She prayed for me a lot, and I have no doubt that her prayers helped me survive and to become the person I am now. I know that Dorothy had lots of fun, even if some of it was when she later remembered the stories and retold them. She was part of our family.

I imagine she is in heaven right now, sharing those Dorothy stories with the angels. They probably have their own names to add to the list of mean little boys they helped raise.

We would have done anything in the world for Dorothy, and she felt the same way about us. Dorothy was an example of angels living among us. I know this because she was able to put up with me.

15

It is amazing to see and hear about the things that people do. It is enough to make me wonder, at times, if they have lost all their common sense, or maybe just never had much to begin with. Some things do not require brain surgery, and they can surely make a difference.

This chapter lists some lessons learned and practiced that I believe can make a real difference, no matter how small they may seem.

1. BE PRESENT IN MIND, BODY, AND SPIRIT.
    We have seen it all before. When someone is really *there*—really present and engaged—in the discussion, actively listening, leading or participating, it is obvious. When serving as a leader, it is essential that the mind, body, and spirit be prepared. Like any athletic event, success usually comes from preparation. Luck has nothing to do with it. Hoping-- or worse, counting—on luck, is a guarantee for failure.

2. SAY "THANK YOU".
    Those two words can inspire and empower other people's actions. It is not hard unless you do not want to recognize the work, sacrifice, and contributions of others. No one succeeds alone. A simple "Thank you" can go a long way.

3. CHECK THE ROOM BEFORE THE MEETING.
This sounds so simple. To some it is unnecessary because someone else has that responsibility. However, it is too late when the crowd is gathered and the room set up, but then has to be changed; or the audio-visual presentation is not ready; or when experiencing those momentum-killing "technical difficulties". "No Surprises" ought to always be the standard and goal of the day.

4. PUT THINGS BACK IN THEIR PROPER PLACE.
Have you ever walked into a room looking for something, knowing where it *should* be, only to discover that it is not there? It can be very frustrating, not to mention a big time-waster. One way to prevent both is by putting things back where they belong when you are finished with them. It sounds so simple; but when it is not done, it creates a self-made frustration point.

5. DO NOT BURN BRIDGES.
This one is easier said than done. It takes a lot of discipline to avoid the temptation of firing back, either with words or actions, just to get back at someone who has hurt or angered you; but such decisions almost always come back to haunt because eventually we may need to cross into that same territory, but past actions or words may have destroyed any chance of future partnerships. This is not to suggest running away from confrontation; but try to leave a thread, a path to reconnect. It can go a long toward making a return trip less awkward and less painful.

6. IF IT'S NOT POSITIVE…DON'T SAY IT.
Again, this is easier said than done. However, this should not be confused with providing constructive input. Our moms

were right when they said to hold our tongues instead of lashing out. Words, once spoken, cannot be taken back and are rarely forgotten or truly forgiven. I have never understood the childhood rhyme about sticks and stones breaking bones, but words never hurting. In my life, words have left deeper scars than sticks or stones ever could.

7. SERVING OTHERS WORKS.

There is a program developed in Columbus by the Pastoral Institute called the Servant Leadership Program. Columbus State University developed it into a certified course. The basic premise is to serve others first, which certainly is not a new concept but one that is an often overlooked. We are conditioned to think and act about ourselves first, believing we deserve this and that above the needs of all others. Little things like letting other folks eat first or letting others be first in line can be revealing. Giving of ourselves to benefit others is not only rewarding but can be transformative for ourselves, as well as for those we serve. A lot of Bible scripture tells about the focus and commands of serving others.

8. POLICIES AND PROCEDURES ARE NOT MULTIPLE CHOICE.

A policy is put into place for the benefit of the whole group. Real problems can occur when a few people decide to pick and choose which rules to follow. I once had an employee that liked to park in spaces reserved for volunteers. The message that it sent was that while all other employees were expected to use designated staff parking spaces, this person was different; the rules did not apply to that person. On the surface, this might seem insignificant; but it set a tone that there was a double standard. Such misconceptions can poison a team, an office, or an organization, corroding it from the inside because, sure enough, others start to pick and choose the policies and rules they deem important enough to follow. It can tear at the fabric of teamwork and team spirit.

9. ALWAYS MAKE THE BOSS LOOK GOOD.
    We all have a boss. Sometimes work is done on his/her behalf, and they seem to show up just in time for the celebration. Call it respect for the office or for the position, but finding positive things to say never hurts. Unfortunately, I have also experienced the opposite from volunteers and staff. It does not take long to hear what people are saying publicly versus what they are saying privately. I once had an employee who agreed with me on a decision in private; but when the execution phase was to begin, they attempted to discredit the decision by saying it was not what they would have done, but were, instead, just going along with it. If you cannot support the BOSS, then find another job.

10. NEVER DO ANYTHING ILLEGAL, IMMORAL, OR UNETHICAL.
    In the world that we live in, crossing the line can feel acceptable, almost expected. After all, everybody does it! It is unfortunate when people in leadership positions recklessly do and say things that do not pass the Smell Test. It seems as if some folks never get caught crossing the line. Sometimes, otherwise innocent bystanders or team members can be pulled across that line as well. I have made some bad decisions, and some in retrospect, that I would not make today; but never have I ever crossed the line of being illegal, immoral, or unethical. It is comforting, at least to me, to know that in spite of differences and disagreements, I can sleep at night knowing that I never crossed those lines.

11. BAD NEWS DOES NOT GET BETTER WITH AGE.
    Unlike a good wine, bad news does not age well. Waiting and hoping usually do not work for the best in the long run. As children, many of us experienced the fear of telling the truth about something, while we hoped our parents would not find out about it; but when they did, the "pain and suffering" was usually much worse because we did not tell them *before* they found out. Also, doing damage control as soon as possible requires much less time, energy, and output than waiting until after the fact.

16

I Quit the Band...AGAIN!

We Gaymons never shied away from the spotlight. Music has always been a part of our lives. Much of it was due to my parents and their love and desire to sing, hear music, and perform; and growing up in the church, there was always music around us.

Mom has played the piano for as long as I can remember. Our family sang every chance we got, and there were lots of chances. Dad, the pastor of the church, always knew he could get the family to sing one of those good old songs to get the congregation actively involved.

My brother played the guitar, while Mom played the piano. Dad usually took the lead because nobody could do it quite like he wanted it done. He decided the tempo and the number of verses to be sung.

We were a born-quartet. Dad sang lead. Hal sang bass and baritone. Mom sang alto, and I was the tenor…and until my voice changed, I could soar right on up there with the best of them. Some of my favorite songs to sing were "In the Valley He Restoreth My Soul", "Who Am I?", and "Through It All".

We performed every week at almost every church service where Dad was the minister or at some other church or event where there was any singing. When people came to our house to visit, the family would gather around the piano and sing. Then, I would be expected to play the piano and sing a song or two.

Dad lives to entertain; and we did it often. We still do! Any time he and Mom come to visit, there will be singing; but now it is the girls who do most of it. However, Dad, at the age of 89, is still up there leading the family in song.

Singing in the family quartet as a tenor was not enough, so Mom decided it would be good for me to learn to play an instrument. Back in those days, we did what our parents asked—or told—us to do, no back talk, no questions. So, in the seventh grade, I took a musical aptitude test and eventually decided to study the cornet, which I liked because it was responsible for the melody of almost all the songs.

Mom worked out a payment plan to buy it. She knew better than to discuss money for things that were not "essential" with Dad, which is still the case today. He came through The Great Depression in a family of seven children, and he still lives like it is the 1930's. I knew that it was going to take some sacrifice for them to come up with the money, which was always scarce for anything beyond the essentials. To this day, I do not know how they did it, but they bought that cornet for me.

Learning to play "the horn", as Dad referred to it, was not hard for me. I guess all those years of being around music just gave me an ear for it. Also, I was extra motivated because no one in the family or in Dad's church could play a horn; so it gave me the chance to shine all by myself. As I said in the beginning, we Gaymons never shied away from the spotlight.

We moved that year to the country, only about five miles out of town, where I attended Mayewood High School. The band director was Dale Graybill, a short, kind of "fleshy" fellow, as my Granddad would say. Dale could play any instrument in that band room and play it well.

I progressed pretty quickly "through the chairs" of the horn section; and in a couple of years, I was sitting in first chair. That was a big deal because the cornets/trumpets lead most of the songs and drove the melody.

Mr. Graybill demanded excellence, even during practice. No matter what else was going on in school, after school, or outside of school, he expected his band to be the best. I wanted to be the best, too. The trouble was that at that age, I had other things on my mind besides playing the horn—specifically girls, football, and church---did I mention girls? How Mr. Graybill could expect so much time to be devoted to practicing music when there were all these other things demanding my time was beyond me.

One afternoon in that old band room, which was way out by the football field, Mr. Graybill pulled out the piece of music, which the band would be playing in a concert in a couple of months. After only a few measures, he stopped the band, which he often did, and called on the horn section to play alone so he could hear us without the support of the rest of the band. It was his cruel and unusual punishment for the kids, like me, who had not really been practicing like we should have been.

When I could not play the piece like he wanted, he called me out, took the horn, and played it perfectly, proving that practice and preparation really do make perfect. Then, he gave it back to me, walked back to the front of the band room, and told us to get out another piece of music. I was totally humiliated in front of the whole band by Dale, who did not have a life other than music…but I DID!

On the way home that afternoon from driving the school bus, I decided that I had had enough of Mr. Graybill and the band. I had other things on which to focus my time, and this band thing was not that important after all; so I decided on my reasons to tell Mom that I was ready to quit.

After working up the nerve to tell Mom, she listened before saying, "Well, do you think Mr. Graybill was right when he said that you just had not practiced enough and that you could do it?" I hated it when she brought reality right back to my face! Of course, she was right, and so was Mr. Graybill. So that night, I pulled out the horn and practiced the piece until I had memorized it.

The next day I was ready. I felt like Clint Eastwood in *Dirty Harry*, telling the bad guys, "Go ahead; make my day." I could hardly wait for Mr. Graybill to pull out the concert piece with which he had embarrassed me the day before, so I could show him how to play it.

We practiced and practiced, but we never did play the concert piece that day. Instead, I just sat there with my horn loaded, waiting for my moment to shine…but the moment never came.

It took a few years and more than a few hard-won lessons, that had nothing to do with music, to appreciate what Mr. Graybill did. He knew that I had the ability; and if I applied my talents, I could be one heck of a good horn player. However, he also knew that the decision of whether or not to use those natural talents to achieve my potential depended totally upon me! I stayed in the band and even played the French horn when we needed one. Mr. Graybill knew I could do it, and so did I.

Sometimes, quitting, temporarily, is not so bad. The process of getting there is just that…a process. Through the process of deciding to walk away from the band, I realized that, while quitting was an option, it was not the right option. Mr. Graybill had shown me that I had the ability to accomplish a lot of things if only I set my mind to it and pay the price to achieve it. I did that and today I am better for it.

Early on, it was the band; but there have been many things—both in my professional career and in my personal life—where it would have been easier just to quit. However, the process of getting to that point required soul searching, forcing me to ask myself the hard questions. Was I quitting because of my lack of commitment? Was I quitting because it was hard? Or, was I quitting because of something that was totally beyond my control? Many times I came to the same conclusion as I had with Dale Graybill and the band—quitting was an option, but it was not the right one.

Mr. Graybill challenged me to commit the time, energy, and talent necessary to achieve our shared goal. He gave me a foundation that I have relied on for more than 40 years of my professional career, not to mention more life lessons than I can count.

I received a college scholarship to play the horn, thanks to Mr. Graybill. I even played in a rock and roll band and made some good money on weekends playing dances and parties, which helped me with the expenses of staying in college. Without Dale's focus, encouragement, and challenges, my musical skills would not have developed to this point.

Sometimes, it is easier to quit. There are many reasons to justify it; but at the end of the day, the biggest challenge we face is ourselves. Can we? Will we? Should we? It is a decision worth thinking about for lifelong learning.

17

The Holiday Inn Gift

We have all heard that it is more blessed to give than to receive. For many of us, it is much easier to say the phrase than to actually believe it and practice it every day in our professional and personal lives.

The Christian Recorder, a publication of the African Methodist Episcopal Church, published this phrase: "Sticks and stones will break my bones but words will never harm me" back in March of 1862. I am sure that most of us have not had sticks and stones hurt our bodies, but we surely have had plenty of words that have left some scars. Our words can comfort, encourage, and provide hope when sometimes it might seem hopeless.

The excitement of giving and watching the receiver smile or laugh, or cry tears of happiness when he opens the gift is truly unique. In fact, money cannot buy the deep feeling of knowing that your gift made a difference in someone's life, or at least brought a big smile and deep appreciation of thanks.

Do you remember the words from the song, "It's Only Words", recorded by the Bee Gees in 1968? The song says that words are "all they have to take the heart away". Powerful and very true. Our words can be more soothing than any medicine that we can take. Our words can be impactful and plant seeds of encouragement beyond our ability to fully comprehend.

Traveling was an enjoyable part of my job with the chamber of commerce. Recruiting new businesses provided all kinds of challenges and opportunities. It was exciting to be able to win "the deal" and to be in competition with other cities, states, and countries. New jobs and new capital investment meant a lot to the new employees and also to the local governments that would benefit from an increased tax base.

When returning from a recruiting trip, we encountered one of those spring pop-up thunderstorms. The Columbus airport is located about 100 miles south of Atlanta International Airport, and some of the flights at that time were in smaller planes, not the regional jets that are now used.

Flying around the storms was similar to the worst roller coaster ride that I have ever had. We were up and down and side to side, to the point that I actually found the "barf bag" in the pocket of the seat just in case I needed it.

We finally landed after a short, but sickening trip. I am sure that I looked like I was already preparing for St. Patrick's Day from the green skin that I was wearing. Once on the ground, I called my wife, Sheila, to tell her that we had landed after a terrible trip and that I was as "sick as a dog".

Unfortunately, I had committed to give a speech that night at the Airport Holiday Inn. Sheila asked me how I was going to do it since I was airsick. I told her that I had eaten some saltine crackers and had drunk some ginger ale; and I thought I would be able to do it in a little while. Also, at this late time, I just could not call the person in charge and tell him that I was sick and unable to do it. Besides, I figured that after I started speaking, the adrenaline would take over. Thank goodness, I was right.

The crowd was very receptive. Once a few laughs began and the eye contact became apparent, it was on! You can usually tell whether you are connecting with the majority of folks or not. I guess it is what my dad, who preached for over 50 years, often went through on Sunday mornings.

Early into the talk, I noticed that one of the servers was standing in the back of the room, listening. It was certainly all right with me, but usually the servers would leave the room and not return until the meeting was over. He stood in the back of the room for the whole presentation.

When the speech was over, the emcee thanked me by presenting me with a gift, as well as offering some kind words. As I was getting my portfolio to leave, the waiter in the back of the room came up to me and asked if I had a couple of minutes to talk. I told him that I did, and that is when the highlight of the day for me really took place.

The server began by saying that he was not supposed to be working that day and night; but someone had gotten sick, and he was called to come in to work. He then said that he had been having a rough time. Lately, he had been having some crazy thoughts about taking his life and that some things that had happened had really knocked him to his knees. As he continued to pour out his heart about the tough times he had been having, I found myself getting caught up in his story. Realizing that I was really the one who was blessed, I felt very thankful.

The man said he was really glad that he had been called to come to work because when he was taking plates off the table, he heard me say that God never makes any junk and that no matter what happens, all of us are wonderfully made. He said those words stopped him in his tracks. While he had been feeling really sorry for himself and wondering if life were worth living, those words kept ringing in his ears.

The young server said he was glad he had decided to listen to the rest of my talk. I thanked him for sharing part of his story with me. Then, I mentioned that I had been traveling that day and had gotten sick earlier from the flight; but after hearing his encouraging words about my talk, I was very glad that I was able to have been there to meet him and hear his story.

There are probably only two of us who remember the events of that night…the server and me. I received a wonderful gift. No, it was not the gift from the organization that hired me to be there, although it was greatly appreciated. My big gift came from someone who inspired me. It came from someone who was not giving a speech that night. Instead, the young man was giving some words of encouragement of his own. There have been lots of talks since then, but few will be remembered like that one.

I received a gift that night at the Airport Holiday Inn that continues to give. It reminds me that, IF POSSIBLE, we need to do whatever we can do to live up to our commitments. More importantly, we never know when something we say or do, no matter how small it may seem, just might be what was needed to make a real difference in someone's life.

It is not about the breaths we take, but maybe it is more about the moments that take our breath away. That night, after my speech, I had my breath taken away. What a wonderful gift I received at the Holiday Inn!

18

I Just Want to be a Blessing

Being a preacher's kid in the Deep South meant I knew what I would be doing on the fifth Saturday night whenever it rolled around...going to a "singing convention" at the church where Dad pastored.

People started gathering around 7 o'clock for fellowship, so they could talk about who was sick, who was in the hospital, and how the crops were doing. It was also a good time for a teenage boy to check out the teenage girl singers performing that night.

Our family always performed during the singings. Since I also played the cornet, Dad thought that it was a good idea for me to play "the horn" during congregational songs and often for the special music when the offering was being taken. I really enjoyed doing it. Mom played the piano, and she was easy to follow. Dad would rather sing than eat, so we sang every chance there was a stage and a congregation.

One of the local favorite groups around those parts of South Carolina was the Welch Family. There were five who sang, played guitars, and keyboard. Mr. Welch played the lead guitar, with his son CG backing him up. The lead vocalist was named Runette. She had a voice that was out of this world and a spirit about her that matched it.

I think Hal and she had a crush on each other. I never could actually catch them holding hands or kissing, but I just knew that there was something going on…you know how little brothers can imagine things.

To be truthful, I kind of liked Dianne, the youngest Welch Family sister. She was so shy that I could hardly even get her to say hello. She was cute and sweet, but I did not figure that she would be able to adjust to the preacher's kid and his style of flirting.

Being a Free Will Baptist of the Pentecostal Faith, shouting, hand-clapping, and speaking in tongues were regular expressions when the Spirit fell down on certain folks. I had read the Bible, so I knew that speaking in tongues was a gift; but I never really understood why some would do it while others would not. If you listened closely, you could tell it was some kind of language, which was sometimes interpreted, which is also a gift.

Anyway, we had some special groups who traveled through in their buses and set up their own speakers and microphones. We knew they were big-time singers when they had 8-track tapes to sell after their performances.

At every singing, Dad called on cousin Lizzy to sing. I do not think she was actually our cousin, but that was all I ever heard her called…Cousin Lizzy Chandler. Every time Dad called on her to sing, she stood in the aisle of her pew and said, "Well, Rev. Freddie, I haven't had a chance to practice, but I want to be a blessing. Y'all pray for me."

Oh, I prayed all right. I prayed that she would not sing; and if she did, I prayed that it would not be the same song that I had heard her sing at least a hundred times.

As she made her way to the piano for Mom to accompany her, she would say again, "I want to be a blessing. Y'all pray for me." Then, the words starting coming out of her mouth. They were the words that I had prayed to never hear again…"He's coming again." Now, I am not really making fun of Cousin Lizzy because the Lord knows she was willing to sing when called upon; but her unique, shrill voice made the fillings in your teeth ache. She always sang all the verses;

but mercifully, that was the only song she must have known because I never heard her sing another one in all those years of singings.

Every time she made her way up, I always thought, "If you really want to be a blessing, why don't you do some practicing and learn another song? You've got time because you know—everyone knows—that Dad's going to call on you to sing."

Later in my life, I have thought about Cousin Lizzy often; and I have even gotten pretty good at imitating her voice and the song she always sang. It is one of those things that we do when Dad and Mom have company or when we get the family together, and Dad insists on entertaining folks.

Now, when I think of that phrase, "I just want to be a blessing", I smile. Then, I am reminded that if I truly want to be a blessing, what am I doing to prepare myself?

I have seen lots of people who want to encourage or inspire others, but there does not seem to be much preparation or hard work to make the situation present itself. Just *wanting* to be a blessing is not enough.

My DNA tells me that there is no substitute for hard work. You pay the price for success. There are no silver spoons, or no such thing as good luck. There is only a lot of preparation, so when the opportunity presents itself you are ready to be a blessing.

19

Some Common Threads of Effective Leadership

I have listened to many speeches and conversations from various leaders during my career. Some of the most memorable ones came from a statement made during a casual conversation, or an "off the cuff remark". This chapter is a summary of many of these conversations. I don't remember who actually said many of these comments since they have been compiled over many years on note pads and put into a file so that the statement would be remembered. Perhaps who said them is not as important as to what was said anyway.

Hopefully, many of these will be useful to put into the reader's "tool box' when leading through a situation or planning for a deliberate strategy in moving forward.

*VISIONING IS VERY IMPORTANT. However, a vision without compelling reasons for taking the present state to a future state will probably fall short. The Bible clearly states that without a vision, the people perish. I suggest that without a vision, the company, the organization, the community will perish. But vision alone will not sustain until the idea becomes a reality. Eventually, the vision must be supported by substance and measurable results.

*CREATING A SENSE OF URGENCY CAN BE TRANSFORMATIVE. When the parameters are challenging, but reachable, this sense of urgency explodes with energy and focus.

One does not have to wait until the building is on fire but having some smoke signals can create a sense of business as usual is simply not going to work.

*DOWNSIZING OFTEN INCLUDES A REDUCTION IN THE WORKFORCE BUT NOT THE WORKLOAD. Good leaders figure out how to accomplish both. Doing more with less is something we all have experienced. Sometimes by working smarter rather than harder, we can accomplish more in quality and quantity.

*CONNECTIVITY AND EMPATHY ARE ESSENTIAL. People don't really care how much you know until they know how much you care. Most folks want to know that there is a real sense of caring and that the employee isn't just another asset to be used. Once there is a real connectivity, then the employee will probably contribute more because they want to and not because they have to do so.

*ALWAYS PROTECT THE INTEGRITY OF THE ORGANIZATION. Integrity usually takes a long time and lots of resources to build. It can be lost quickly. A good leader never forgets and will always stand in the gaps protecting and fighting for the integrity of the entity.

*BE TRUE TO YOURSELF AND TO YOUR MORALS AND VALUES. At the end of the day, the greatest challenge that we face is who we see in the mirror. Being able to not only look at yourself but accept the person that you see is extremely important. While leaders can modify their positions and revamp their approach, in the end, you must draw the line as to what you will think and do and what you will not.

*LEVERAGE YOUR UNIQUENESS AND THAT OF THE PEOPLE AROUND YOU. We are all wonderfully made but packaged differently. This uniqueness can be the key to competing and winning. It can be challenging at times, but well worth the effort.

*MOTIVITATIONAL TALK IS NOT ENOUGH. There must be measurable outcomes that track expectations. Giving a timely and good "pep talk" is sometimes what the team needs and usually can bring about some instant results. The old saying about a picture being worth a thousand words is still applicable and very appropriate. Showing the team, as well as telling the team, go hand and hand.

*BE SURE TO THINK TACTICALLY AND STRATEGICALLY. Winning the battle while losing the war is not a sustainable strategy. Developing a good game plan requires a look at many options and many scenarios. Too many times emotion and egos take over and action is then taken. Victories can occur for sure. A short term victory quickly loses its appeal when challenges keep coming; and the leader has to find the energy and resources to fight them. Some of these battles can be prevented or at least lessened with the proper thought process being taken in advance.

*THE BEST COACHING HAPPENS BEFORE AND AFTER THE GAME AND NOT JUST DURING THE GAME. We have all witnessed a ball game where one specific play call made the difference in the game. Most games are won by the preparation that goes into them before they ever start. Being mentally prepared before the situation ever presents itself takes preparation. A good leader is forever coaching the team. Learning from good and not so good examples can prepare the individual members for the next scenario when they must contribute to the overall success.

*PREPARATION, HARD WORK AND EXECUTION USUALLY EQUAL SUCCESS. Most people want to win. Most people enjoy the benefits of being on a winning team. The real winning happens every day. How the leader challenges and empowers the team members to prepare and then execute makes a big difference in the amount of success that occurs. Most success takes hard work. Becoming successful is a challenge, but staying successful is a commitment.

*20%-60%-20% - When new ideas or changes are announced, 20% of the workforce will jump on board immediately. Another 20% will resist it, will hate the change and probably won't ever truly get fully on board. Meanwhile, 60% will be part of the progress if they are part of the process. Sometimes leaders spend too much energy on trying to get 100% buy in to the process. Perhaps, the focus should be on the 60% that can be lead, persuaded, or encouraged to understand and accept why the idea or change is needed and required.

*MEASUREMENTS SHOULD NOT ALWAYS BE TIED TO COMPENSATION. Evaluations should not occur only during annual review periods. Asking employees to "come to the office" should be a positive experience and not one that the staff fear or hate. A good leader will set the environment where for the most part, the employees know where they stand before an annual evaluation is ever formally conducted. Often, an encouraging word of praise and appreciation will go further with the loyalty of an employee than a small bonus.

*KEEP YOUR EGO IN CHECK. Don't regard yourself too highly. Having confidence in your abilities is essential to being a good leader. There have been too many leaders who let their egos stand in the way of the success of the team. Most of us don't want to be like the situation in the book about the emperor's new clothes when we are walking around in our underwear, thinking that everything is fine when it is not. One way to prevent that from happening is to have a "healthy ego" and not one that is toxic.

*DON'T BELIEVE ALL OF YOUR NEWS CLIPPINGS. We enjoy reading positive things that may be said about our leadership or accomplishments. Encouraging words can be addictive. Leaders surely get their fill of negative comments; however, it is important to keep both the good and the not so good comments in context. Both are usually short lived, so we need to treat both as a moment in time and not as being permanently fixed.

*WE WILL NEVER BE AS GOOD AS WE ARE CAPABLE OF BEING. When we think that we are as good as we can be, then we have stopped growing. There is always room for learning.

Jim Collins' book, *Good to Great,* was correct because as Collins said, most companies do not want to leave the comfort level of their current success by taking risks to get to the next level to become great. We may become good leaders, but can we become great leaders? It is up to us.

*TAKE CARE OF YOURSELF....spiritually, mentally, financially, emotionally, and physically. Some might call this the balance that we all need. Everyone has probably seen examples where leaders were financially at the top of their game. They made the bottom line shine due to their focus and work; but this same person might have died of a heart attack because he/she never took time to go to the gym and exercise the body. We have also seen people who take care of everyone else but neglect themselves or their families. I don't know of any special formulas; but I do know that finding the "right balance" of all of these elements will make us better spouses, parents, friends and leaders.

*TREAT PEOPLE FAIRLY. Terminating employees can be gut wrenching. Knowing that the person tried, but just did not meet the measurements that the job demanded, and a separation ensued causes some real heart burn. Treating people the way we want to be treated is a great guide, no matter what the situation may be.

*FRIENDS WILL COME AND GO BUT ENEMIES WILL ACCUMULATE. True friends are few and far between. We all have "situational friends". They will be our friends when it makes sense for them to be; but when the chips are down and the pressure is on, they may not be around. However, our enemies don't ever seem to go away for good. Like barnacles on a ship, once they get there, they start to attract others to join them for the ride. It is what it is; so instead of worrying too much about them, just be aware that enemies are there in the shadows.

* THE COMMUNICATIONS PROBLEM. George Bernard Shaw said that the single biggest problem in communication is the illusion that it has taken place. There is a big difference in talking

and communicating. All of us have played the game where we whisper something to the person next to us and that person, in turn, whispers to the next person. By the time the message gets back around, it has changed a good bit. Even in written communications, we, as the writers, know what we are saying; but the recipient gets a totally different message than what was intended. Sometimes it is helpful to ask for feedback to ensure that the communication was correctly received and understood.

*LEAPING MONKEYS. Don't let the monkey on someone else's back jump onto yours without bringing possible solutions. Often an employee shares a concern or problem and wants to leave it on your back for you to solve. After all, as the leader you are a problem solver. Unfortunately, the leader becomes the solver, while employees only become the carriers of the news and don't grow into the depth of maturing in problem solving that strengthens them and the organization. Listening to their issues is important. Giving them some suggestions at times can also be helpful; but fixing the problems for them time after time is not helping them to grow and develop as they could and should.

*WHAT STAFF MAY NOT BE UP ON USUALLY FINDS THEM DOWN ON. Inclusion at the right time is healthy and powerful. There is a time to include and a time to exclude different elements of the organization. When it gets to the stage where "buy in" is important and necessary, the timing of their engagement must be a careful consideration. Most people will be in support if they genuinely they feel that they have been informed and included to the degree that makes sense. Top down directives don't usually build support that is sustainable.

*ASK, THEN LISTEN. What do people really think? If you ask them, be prepared to listen. One mistake that leaders make is going through the motions of appearing to want feedback only to have the employees find out that the decision has already been made and the listening exercise of the leader was one of "checking the box".

*GETTING THE CREDIT. It's amazing what happens if you don't care who gets the credit. Getting appropriate recognition is certainly ok. When success happens, many folks will want to take the credit even though, for the most part, they have only been spectators. Giving credit away is powerful. We have all heard the phrase that "There is no I in Team". At times, giving credit to others provides for a synergy that might never occur.

Kessel Stelling was the CEO of SYNOVUS during the time of the TARP funds being loaned to banks in America. This company had a $968 million loan that has since been paid back to the federal government plus interest. Some of his statements during that trying time to employees and the community were:

*It's much easier to lead when things are going well.

*Focus on the things that you can control and have an impact upon.

* Under promise but over deliver.

*Don't believe all the news….it probably not that bad and probably not that good either.

*Short term and long term decisions should be made with the company's culture and best interest in mind.

*IF YOU ARE GOING THROUGH HELL, KEEP GOING. Being a preacher's kid, I grew up hearing, reading and saying the 23rd Psalm. One of the most powerful words in this passage of scripture was found in the 4th verse. "Yea, though I walk THROUGH the valley of the shadow of death….." Through is an extremely encouraging word. We may be in a very difficult situation that is overwhelming, but it won't last forever. Whatever it may seem to be and however stressful it actually is, there will be a day when we will be through it, and we will be looking at it in our rearview mirrors.

*EFFECTIVE MANAGEMENT IS ABOUT DOING THE THINGS RIGHT. EFFECTIVE LEADERSHIP IS ABOUT DOING THE RIGHT THING. Many times haste brings about waste. Effective management makes sure that we understand the mission and how to accomplish it before we spend resources. Effective leadership ensures that we don't just execute but that we are doing the right thing by executing. Maybe it is the black and white of things. If it is wrong today, it will probably be wrong tomorrow.

*TRUE LEADERSHIP IS AN INVISIBLE STRAND, AS MYSTERIOUS AS IT IS POWERFUL. Leadership pulls and it bonds. It is a catalyst that creates unity out of disorder. It is like the rudder on a ship that steers towards the destination. Sometimes it is behind the curtain and sometimes it is out front. You can't buy it or take something to enhance it. Leadership is a continual process of learning, executing and energizing the followers to keep moving forward.

*THE ROAD TO THE NEXT HILL IS ALWAYS UPHILL. Being a successful leader takes work and sacrifice. In order to achieve new heights there have to be challenges of moving upwards. These challenges require energy, commitment, and resources, both personal and professional.

* A GOOD LEADER MUST HAVE P.R.I.D.E. Personal Responsibility In Delivering Excellence. The "buck stops here" is another way of saying this. We too often see leaders who want to blame someone else instead of accepting responsibility. Frankly, I grow tired of some elected officials who seem to always find someone else to blame rather than to accept the responsibility for their office that they have been elected to serve. The public sector is not the only place where this way of ducking responsibility is found. In good times and bad times, a good leader steps up and accepts the responsibility, rather than finding excuses or reasons to have alibis.

*WHETHER YOU THINK YOU CAN OR WHETHER YOU THINK YOU CAN'T, YOU ARE RIGHT! It is a matter of attitude. Have you ever heard someone say something like, "I knew it wasn't going to work". Often, our perspectives become reality if our thinking is not clear and focused on the ultimate goals.

*I DON'T KNOW THAT IF THINGS CHANGE THAT THEY WILL BE BETTER. We need to be careful in presenting false expectations. Sometimes our crystal ball becomes cloudy, and what we thought would happen may have unintended consequences. One thing that we can say that has been tried, tested and proven: "I do know that if things are to get better, they must change".

*GROW ANTENNAS AND NOT HORNS. It is important to be able to have people, internally and externally, who are not afraid to approach the leader with a suggestion, input or idea. One way to cut off two way communication is to have an environment of hostility or unwelcomed input. A good way to help with the adversarial element is to listen and to have a dialog, when appropriate, instead of an absolute set-in-stone way. My grandmother used to say that honey catches more bees than vinegar, and I think she was right.

*RECOGNIZE WHEN TO QUIT. Leaders must be able to assess the situation and determine when it is time to get on a different path. If insanity is doing the same thing the same way and expecting different results, then stopping the bleeding of resources so that we are able to fight another day is sometimes the best strategy. It's OK to say that something simply didn't work out like we had planned. I always use more erasers on my pencils than I do the lead anyway, don't you?

*PEOPLE WANT TO KNOW.....Can I trust you? Trust is at the foundation of any relationship. Personal or professional relationships can be won or lost depending on the trust that is present or absent. If I don't trust you to be honest in all situations, then I have to try to decide when you *are* being honest and when you *are not*. Once trust is broken, it is very difficult to ever build it back to where it once was. If an employee trusts that his/her best interest is always going to be considered, that trust will go a long way to working through difficult and challenging situations. I used to hear some military guys make the statement about who they would want in the foxhole with them. While we aren't usually engaged in life and death like this military example, it should be worth our asking the question to make sure that there are no doubts, as far as the trustworthiness of the person with whom we are working.

*INVEST IN YOUR PEOPLE….train them, empower them, provide feedback to them, and recognize them. Simply asking them about their child's ball game or dance recital can be worth a lot to them. My son mentioned to us that the big supervisor came into the bathroom at work not long ago and called him by his first name. Then, he went on to have a conversation about some of his work experiences and skills. Before leaving, he mentioned that he might want to talk with him again about something new that was being considered. It only cost the supervisor a little time to know something about my son and his work background and to make a point of engaging directly with him. I probably don't have to tell you what it meant to Wes. We can invest in people in many different ways. If we continue to look at our time, talent and resources as an investment, then we will probably see returns on those investments beyond our imaginations.

*MAKE SURE THAT YOU HAVE THE BIG IDEAS RIGHT. There is nothing worse than a brand of the week. Here is a new initiative that we are going to try, and we want everyone to get behind it. Big ideas deserve some big planning and big roll outs. We have only one chance at the first impression. Setting expectations high can be greatly accelerated by making sure that the big idea is the right one from the beginning until the end.

*GENERATE A UNITY OF EFFORT. We know that a house divided will not be able to stand and sustain itself. We don't have to worry about getting 100% consensus buy in but we should strive to get 100% to be agreeable to the process of inclusion to develop the final decision. "We vs. they" speaks volumes about the organization's leadership. We have all heard comments like, "they say". Who is they? Perhaps "they" is them.

*PURSUE THE ENEMY RELENTLESSLY. These enemies are anything that tear down the organization and its values and culture. They could be those who think they are so special that they don't have to park in the designated parking spaces; or someone who thinks he/she is too busy to attend the meeting; or a person who takes pot shots at the leader, trying to plant doubt in the minds of others about their leadership abilities. Sometimes the enemy is outside the organization, but sometimes the enemy is within. If left alone in hopes that things will get better, the enemy will grow in strength and become even a bigger force to deal with down the road.

*EXERCISE INITIATIVE. Being proactive and seeking ways to get the job done is what separates the winners from all the others. In 1970, the spacecraft Apollo 13, the seventh manned mission, was to be the third to land on the moon. Because of an explosion that deprived most of the oxygen supply and electric power, the mission had to be aborted. Due to the training on earth that had been done previously, as well as actual trial by error repairs during the mission, the problems were overcome; and the three astronauts, Lovell, Swigert and Haise returned to earth safely. The movie, released in 1995, which grossed over $355 million called the explosion a "success failure".

*IT'S NOT ABOUT YOU. Rick Warren's book about servant leadership starts out with this statement as his first sentence. Too many leaders think that it is about them. Too many employees think that it is about them. Too many politicians think that it is about them. Once you understand and accept that we are instruments put here on earth to serve GOD, things should get into the correct priority. By serving others, we serve our mission.

*NOT MANY THINGS ARE TOTALLY BRAND NEW. Paul Harvey once said, "In times like these we must remember that there will always be times like these". Sure we have new things invented. New ways of solving problems come along often. But good vs evil....solving problems....caring...leading...right and wrong.... have always been and always will be. We have to find ways to learn from the past in order to project a better result for the future.

*THERE ARE LIFTERS AND THERE ARE LEANERS. Lifters make a real difference and are needed to help the leaners by giving them support. There are times when lifting is needed and times when leaning is as well. But leaders find ways to lift far more than they lean.

*BE QUICK TO LISTEN, SLOW TO SPEAK AND SLOW TO ANGER. (James 1:19) Imagine what the world would be like today if everyone practiced this!

*IF AT THE END OF THE DAY THINGS LOOK BAD, BE PATIENT. Many times things will look better in the morning. We all have bad days. We probably all have had some days when we wonder if it is worth the effort to keep trying. We probably all have written the email to get it off our chests and blow off steam but we didn't push the send button. Then, the next morning we read it again and decide it probably doesn't make sense to send it.

*LIFE IS LIKE A MARATHON. Know when to sprint and when to coast, but never stop or the world will pass you by. Sometimes we have to take a moment and breathe. Sometimes getting away from the tasks is the best thing to do. Sometimes we may have to coast and ride downhill for a while. It's all right to pace yourself as a leader. We need to make sure that we will always have enough steam to get up over the next hill and next challenge.

*LEADERS WITH BRAINS, POWER AND RESOURCES ARE COMMON. A competent leader full of integrity and skill, coupled with sincerity, is rare. We all know examples of national leaders who had the power, the brains, and the resources to do some unbelievable things, both good and bad. They are in the history books and living among us in the world today. However, we all probably know of leaders who had those elements, along with integrity and sincerity, as well. Their impact on the world is remarkable. Sometimes their impact wasn't known until after their death; but what a difference they made.

*SOMETIMES REAL LEADERSHIP IS NOT WELCOMED. I had a mentor when I began my chamber career who said that the only way to please everybody was to please some when you came, some while you were there, and the others when you left. Sometimes it is lonely at the top of the organization or business. Sometimes real leadership that is willing to take the risk and bring about change is not welcomed and can be resented. Effective leaders do not lead only when times are good or when the water is calm; instead, real leaders understand that there is no expiration date on leading.

*LEADERS LEAD BY EXAMPLE. When there is a job to be done, look to see where the leader is. I have also heard that you can judge a leader by his/her followers. Many times I have heard people remark about the leader helping to clean up after an event, along with the other staff members. It can help not only to set a tone about what the team is all about, but also what the leader is about, as well. The best example that I can think of is about the Lord's Last Supper. Jesus washed the disciples' feet, not because he had to, but because he wanted to show them what serving others was really all about.

*REAL LEADERS ARE BRIDGE BUILDERS, NOT BRIDGE BURNERS. It takes a long time to build a bridge but it doesn't take too long to tear one down. Tearing down a bridge (relationship) requires very little skill. Building relationships among team members and other leaders takes a lot of time, effort, and energy.

*A DEFINITION OF LEADERSHIP. Leadership is the art of directing and guiding. It is the ship that leads the way. We can learn to be more effective and efficient leaders. Sometimes we learn by example. Often we learn by experiences. As leaders, we must accept the role that we are like the rudder on the boat. It is our job to help steer to the desired location. It is our responsibility to steer through the storms and through the calm. Dad used to say, "I had rather see a sermon than to hear one". Hopefully, we can show what it takes to be a good leader through our thoughts, actions and demonstrated results of leading.

*LEADERSHIP NEVER GIVES UP AND NEVER GIVES OUT. J.W. Fanning, the longest serving advisor for Leadership Georgia, the oldest statewide leadership program in the United States, used to say, "Don't let me die before I am dead." Real leaders are like the Energizer Bunny Rabbit and the Timex watch....they just keep running and running and never give out.

*WHERE IS THE LEADERSHIP ANSWER BOOK? There are many tremendous books on leadership that can help, guide, encourage and challenge us to be all that we can be. Personally, I believe that the Bible contains the values and principles to guide personally and professionally. I have also used books like: *FIRST THINGS FIRST, NO EASY DAY, GOOD TO GREAT, SIMPLE STEPS TO IMPOSSIBLE DREAMS, THE BE HAPPY ATTITUDES and WINNING EVERYDAY* as good resources to find some of the possible answers to questions and perspectives that might be a good fit for the decisions that need to be made.

*BE FULLY PRESENT. Physically being there is of course obvious. However, being engaged in listening, participating in, and challenging your own bias and thought patterns to see if there are some missing pieces can bring about excitement and freshness. Wayne Gretzky played for 20 years in the National Hockey League from 1979 to 1999. He was nicknamed "The Great one". He has also been called the greatest hockey player that has ever played the game. He is still the leading scorer in NHL history. He was once asked about what made him such a good player. His reply was that he had the ability to skate to where the puck was going to be. You can't anticipate and be where you need to be unless you are fully present in every respect.

*LEADERSHIP BY COMMITTEE. It has been said that a camel was a horse that was created by a committee. Committees can provide great insight and can be a tremendous asset to the process. One of the challenges is to make sure that the proper checks and balances are in place with parameters so that this group of people doesn't forget the main objective of the purpose of their being together. If Moses had a committee, then he would have written the 10 suggestions instead of the commandants.

*THERE ARE THREE WAYS TO GUARANTEE FAILURE: 1. thinking that you are always right; 2. thinking that people who don't support you are bullheaded and stupid; and 3. thinking that a turtle got up on the fence post by itself.

*YOU CAN CHANGE THE COURSE OF HISTORY EASIER THAN YOU CAN CHANGE A HISTORY COURSE. There are always reasons, excuses, hurdles, and egos that will try to keep you from succeeding. When working with universities, I have found that many times they can be so set in their ways and so engrained in how they do things that change is met with great resistance, often from the tenured professors. There are, of course, exceptions to the rules. Columbus Technical College, Georgia's Quick Start Program, and Columbus State University have demonstrated why they are exceptions. While we were working to meet specific workforce needs of TSYS, the world's leading financial processing company during Y2K, one of the department heads at Georgia Tech was brought in to see if he could help address the specific computer programming and processing needs for the company. It became pretty obvious during the meeting that his answers were coming from his world of academics and not the world in which TSYS was competing everyday around the world. The then Chancellor of the Board of Regents made the statement, "You can change the course of history easier than you can change a history course." Immediately, it became obvious that the Chancellor was a problem solver who was way out of the typical institutional box. The rest of the story is that a special initiative was put in place using both of the institutions mentioned above and the workforce needs of TSYS were met. That issue became one for the history books and is not a current challenge.

*LEADERS ARE BORN TO WIN BUT WE ARE CONDITIONED TO LOSE. In today's times, it appears that some of the politically correct type of folks want everyone to win. While I understand some of that reasoning, life is not about everyone winning or losing. I believe that by losing, we learn how to win. Let's face it, life can be pretty rough at times. When the times get hard, that is probably when we can grow the most. Refusing to lose and trying again and again is what makes good leaders examples to follow.

*BEING LUCKY. Bill Russell was one of the most famous basketball players of his day. As a player, the teams he played on were 11 times NBA champions; he was the NBA Most Valuable Player 5 times and was selected to be on the NBA All –Star Team 12 different times. Needless to say, Russell earned his recognitions. When asked about being lucky, he often replied, something to the effect that he did not know about luck; but he did know that it is very unlucky to be behind at the end of the game. I believe to a large degree we make our own luck.

*OUR ATTITUDE GOVERNS OUR ALTITUDE. There are many tremendous examples of people who fought the odds with physical handicaps, terrible home life, poverty, and many other things that most folks never have to encounter. Yet, in spite of all of these, they became very successful people. Some by becoming multi-millionaires, some by impacting millions of people through their service to humanity and some by becoming an icon in their own fields of service. Heather Whitestone, former Miss Alabama, lost her hearing at the age of eighteen months. When asked about what she thought was one of the greatest handicaps in life, she replied that negative thinking was on the top of her list and that people handicap themselves by concentrating only on the negative instead of the positive. In 1994, she competed in the Miss America Pageant and won.

Made in the USA
Charleston, SC
08 November 2015